Animals Speak!

By

Betty Lewis, RVT, Dr. A.N.

Illustrations by Verne K. Foster

ISBN: 0-75962-172-1

This book is printed on acid free paper.

1stBooks - rev. 3/2/01

Disclaimer

The information in this book is meant to educate readers about telepathic communication with animals and related holistic topics. There is no intent to suggest that these techniques should replace the care of an animal's health care provider.

In most cases, the names of the humans and animals are fictitious. Their stories, however, are real.

Table of Contents

Acknowledgements.. vii
Introduction ix

Part I

Chapter 1 Animals Speak! About Companionship..................... 1
Chapter 2 Animals Speak! About Telepathy for Healing.......... 17
Chapter 3 Animals Speak! About Behavior 37
Chapter 4 Animals Speak! About Training 47
Chapter 5 Animals Speak! About Grief.................................... 53
Chapter 6 Animals Speak! About Things Out of this World..... 61
Chapter 7 Animals Speak! About the Ten Commandments of
            Living with Animals.. 69

Part II

Chapter 8 What is Telepathy?.. 75
Chapter 9 Exercises in Telepathy 81
Chapter 10 The Steps.. 87
Chapter 11 Loose Ends.. 93

Appendix I   Vaccinations/
               Nutrition/Training/Grooming/Environment 99
Appendix II   Nutrition (again) 103
Appendix III   The Predator/Prey Relationship....................... 121
Appendix IV   Cleaning Up Your Act 123
Appendix V   Resources... 125

Acknowledgements

An author gets credit for the writing of a book, and, indeed, it is my creation. However, without the input and encouragement of many individuals, I would not have had the impetus to make it happen.

My sincere thanks go to:

Beatrice Lydecker, Animal Communicator. Bea introduced me to the concept of talking with animals telepathically and taught me how to do it.

Virginia Kirmayer Slayton, editor and publisher of *Convergence* magazine. Many of the stories in the book first appeared in *Convergence* and several times over the many years of our association, Ginny asked me "When are you going to turn these into a book?" The answer is, finally, "Now."

Michele Masterfano. I met Michele on the Internet. Michele took on the huge task of helping me to organize my thoughts and my *Convergence* columns. She then proof-read the book several times, catching typographical errors and asking pertinent questions to help me to clarify what I wanted to say.

The heart-wrenching story of Michele and Sheba appears in the Health Chapter.

Laurie Blakeney, editor extraordinaire. Laurie's attention to detail and clear editing style made the seemingly formidable task of editing the book a pleasure. Her accessibility and warm encouragement pushed the book to its final form.

Bill Lewis, my husband and best friend. Bill has always said, "You can't win if you don't play." Even when it meant he had to stay home and "hold down the fort," Bill encouraged me to go out and do my thing. Thank you, Bill, for making it possible for me to play.

And, of course, my heartfelt thanks to all the animals who have been my greatest teachers.

viii

Introduction

Many people think the ability to talk to animals is a special gift given only to a few people. I believe it's a special gift, all right, but it's given to all people!

I'm frequently asked, "when did you first know you could talk to the animals?" "Did you do it as a child?" Many seem to think that it might be too late for them!

My story isn't dramatic, but perhaps that's the beauty of it! I *wasn't* a child prodigy. I was the product of a prosaic, middle class family. Yet, I'm now a professional animal communicator! If I can do it, anyone can. Maybe my story will help inspire confidence in those who want to remember this skill that accompanies all of us into this world.

In childhood, I had a few dogs, assorted fish and some turtles. I also remember a parakeet who was with us a few years. I wasn't "remarkable" in any particular way, however. When it came to animals, I enjoyed nature and walks in the woods. I learned some animals' tracks, to recognize some birdsongs, and to know a few star constellations. Many of our family vacations were camping ones, but animals didn't spring to life under my magic care, nor did parades of animals follow me home.

It wasn't until I was in my 30's, having made a commitment to the Great Dane breed and the Veterinary Technician profession, that I became aware that telepathic communication with other animal species was possible and that I could do it.

My first introduction to the concept was when I read Beatrice Lydecker's book called *What the Animals Tell Me.* I was intrigued and saw tremendous possibilities for its uses in my life ranging from it just being plain "fun" to having practical application in the veterinary hospitals where I worked. In the book, Bea describes how she learned to talk with animals and tells the reader how to do it too. Maybe I did pick up a little from the book, but not enough to feel that I was really "doing it". In 1979, Bea was part of a program I attended in Missouri. I went to the seminar, hoping for a breakthrough, but still the real ability to talk to animals eluded me.

As part of my husband's Air Force career, we had the privilege of living in a variety of places. In 1981, we were living in Fresno, CA. As luck would have it, Bea Lydecker had moved and was living in Los Angeles at the time. Cosmic forces were coming together. It was in her living room that I finally had my "Ah ha" experience.

It had been a long day. Twenty-five tired people and dogs were bringing the workshop to a close when Bea asked us to ask Charlie, a Samoyed who his favorite friend was. An instant picture of a turtle flashed into my mind, but it seemed pretty far-fetched. I remained quiet. No one else said anything either, though, so Bea prompted us: "*Somebody* must have gotten *something*!" I took a deep breath and said, "Well, I saw a turtle..." "That's *it!*" Charlie's person said, "He plays with this large turtle!"

From that moment on, I knew how it felt to receive information from outside of myself. Once you know what it feels like, you can do it again, or at least, recognize the same feeling when it comes again. After that, it's a matter of practice.

My animal educational background is in veterinary medicine. I started working in veterinary practices in 1973, graduated with a degree in Veterinary Technology in 1979 and, during the course of my husband's 20 year Air Force career, worked for 25 veterinarians in 17 different practices in 4 states. During that time, one of the often-repeated comments I heard was "I just wish this animal could *tell* us what is wrong!" Guessing "where it hurts" is sometimes very frustrating, but with animal telepathy it's possible to know!

With the awareness that talking to another species was real came my introduction to holistic medicine. By 1984, I was increasingly aware of some of the limitations of allopathic (what we in the U.S. think of as conventional) medicine. I kept searching for "another way" to approach many of the issues that were so common every day in the veterinary hospital.

Eventually, my solutions were quite different from those I had to advocate in my professional life. That was one of the reasons, in 1987, I left conventional medicine and opened my holistic consulting practice called Paws & Reflect.

Paws & Reflect began as a service to help people better understand animals, particularly their domestic companions, but I quickly learned how important it is to operate within the holistic paradigm. Nothing exists alone; everything interacts. The whole animal, from its nutrition to how it feels about its home life, to its relationships with other pets and people must be considered when trying to solve problems. Each area of concern led me to more study.

I've incorporated a variety of modalities into my approach to health, from diet to herbs to Therapeutic Touch and Reiki to TTEAM (Tellington Touch) and flower essences and am always in the process of learning more. My degree as a Doctor of Naturopathy in 1993 tied together much of my learning. (Some articles in the Appendices of this book will address some of these other topics.)

An important part of my practice lies in referring people to other specialists as well, such as chiropractors, homeopaths and holistic veterinarians.

Most importantly, I've learned to listen to the animals. They can help us to help them and in return, they help us. Together, we can make the world a better place to live.

Chapter I

Animals Speak! About Companionship

R-E-S-P-E-C-T, Tell You What It Means To Animals!

Respect: n. 1. To feel or show esteem for, to honor.
2. To show consideration for, avoid violation of; treat with deference

A man named Joe once called me about his dog Winston who, it turned out, was a highly trained obedience competition dog with whom the man had high hopes of winning in the obedience ring. His problem was that Winston wouldn't work for him. "What," he wanted to know, "was wrong with this dog?" He was trained, after all, he should perform!

Winston was very forthcoming with his answer. "I don't like this guy's attitude," he told me. "He expects me to jump when he says jump and, frankly, I don't see why I should."

Even though we live with animals and hear people talk about their pets as "best friends," or "practically human," we also often get sidetracked by the fact that animals have such different physical shapes from ours. We forget that while there are differences between humans and animals, there really are many more similarities. Animals have feelings, too, and the sooner we can step back and see them as individuals, the better our relationships with them will be.

Lack of respect and consideration was at the root of the problem between Winston and Joe. Winston was a competitive being who wanted to be in a partnership but not exhibited as a puppet. When I told my client this, he immediately changed his approach. He "respected'" an individual with this kind of attitude and, in fact, was really like that himself. As soon as he began treating Winston as an equal in performance situations, Winston responded accordingly. Now they are a winning combination.

1

Another similar story involves a friend of mine and her Bloodhound. This time the working relationship was a good one, but the dog actually had been responsible for part of the training.

There is an exercise called "attention" where the dog is supposed to follow, with her body position, wherever the person's eyes go. For example, if the handler looks right, the dog moves into position so she can sit and see the eyes. If the person now looks back to the left, the dog moves backwards, always watching the handler's eyes. This particular dog caught on quickly and thought it was a fun game (it's certainly impressive to watch!) One day, during the game, the handler got distracted and looked away. Immediately she was "corrected" by a loud bark as the dog chastised her for breaking training! The handler learned quickly, too, and now she concentrates on the game until it's over! Mutual respect, mutual training.

I am not suggesting that we treat our animal companions as furry children. Instead, consideration for the emotional and intellectual needs of animals as individuals should be our goal. When we approach all animals, wild or domestic, with respect as the cornerstone, we all benefit from the results.

What telepathy is and what it isn't

The dictionary definition of telepathy is the "transfer of pictures, thoughts, and feelings using mental energy". It's that simple...energy from the sender is converted sometimes into pictures or sounds or smells or thoughts or emotions in the receiver. The entire range of the senses can be used and the intensity depends on the strengths of both the sender and receiver.

For example, dogs have an extraordinary sense of smell. Most dogs will be able to send incredibly explicit olfactory images. People, as a species, are extremely deficient in this sense, but will have their understanding of smells somewhat enhanced by what is being transferred by the dog. On the other hand, humans as a species are generally good visually. Some people will receive very vivid pictures from other beings. For some they come like snapshots, for others it might actually be like watching TV in your head. There's still a range depending on individual strengths.

It is important to realize that communication through telepathy is only a part of the way animals communicate. Mental communication doesn't *replace* body language, which is very highly developed in some species.

Vocalizations are an important part of communication as well. A warning bark, a whine or a yip, all convey different messages as do a meow, yowl or hiss. The more communication cues available to two individuals, the more complete the communication.

Another common misconception is that through telepathy we can "make" an animal do something. An animal who won't respond to an English word she knows (such as asking a dog to "come" to you) is not necessarily more likely to come just because you are talking in her "native" language.

However, you do make the request that much *clearer* to the animal when you add the telepathy factor! With understanding might come compliance.

The advantages of being able to have two way conversations with animals are numerous. The reason most of us share our lives with animals is for companionship; telepathic communication enhances companionship with all beings. Being able to pinpoint health concerns is an extremely good reason for learning this skill, as is the ability to resolve behavioral differences of opinion. Telepathy can clarify confusion in training situations, making the learning of "house manners" a breeze and infusing exhilaration into formal or competitive training situations. The area of pre-grief counseling and grief counseling for animals and humans are other times when telepathic communication excels as well. These topics will all be covered in later chapters in detail.

Hazel & Me

One of the things I discovered once I began exploring the world of interspecies telepathic communication was that many animals have a terrific sense of humor. Some animals are total hams, living life with a gleeful bound a smile and a will to make you laugh. Anyone can recognize the fun-loving attitude of these animals, but there are many others with a dry or droll sense of humor which is not obvious to most people. Take the story of my friend Hazel, a fawn colored Great Dane.

I was driving one of my own dogs, Libby, to the home of her professional handler. She was going off with him on a circuit to Oklahoma in a search for what are called "majors" in dog show parlance. These are large shows which convey large numbers of points towards a championship.

A friend of mine asked me to take her dog, Hazel, to the handler as well. Hazel was already a champion and was being shown as a Special, or in Best of Breed competition, the stepping stone to Group and Best in Show wins. Hazel had done well in the show ring and was obviously highly motivated to show. There was no question that she loved it.

Hazel was riding in a crate behind the driver's seat and was a bit agitated by the drive. To calm her, to pass the time for us both and maybe pick up some show tips, I started talking to her.

I asked her questions like "What do you find appealing about showing?" "What's your favorite part of the show scene?" and "How can humans make showing more fun for dogs?" Our conversation went on for some time and then, just as you might glance at a human passenger, I glanced back at Hazel in the crate behind me. Suddenly, the realization hit her that she had been talking to me! She whipped her head around at me and looked me in the eye: "I didn't know *humans* could talk!" she said!

She was so astonished that I burst out laughing. From that time on, though, we were best friends. When she had her puppies a year or so later, I was one of the only people outside of the family members to be allowed to touch them. We remained special friends throughout her life. Not only did we cement a friendship that day, but I gained an appreciation for her dry wit.

Tidy and Carole

A totally different kind of story, but also one where telepathy enhanced interspecies companionship is the story of Tidy, the Bouvier de Flandres and her person, Carole.

Carole came to me in genuine distress. She was afraid that her dog Tidy might want to live with someone else.

Shortly after acquiring Tidy, Carole became very ill. It was all she could do to take care of Tidy's physical needs, let alone give him the emotional support she felt he must need. She felt guilty about "rescuing" Tidy from a poor situation at the age of two years, only to fall down on the job of providing something much better.

Now she was well and she was serious about wanting to know if her dog blamed her for a bad life.

When Tidy heard this, he was horrified and very indignant! "Do you mean to tell me that after all these months of waiting and watching by her bedside and taking care of her, she is thinking of *dumping* me?" he said to us.

Carole was so relieved when she heard this. She *loved* Tidy and the last thing she wanted was to give him up. In fact, she loved him so much that she was willing to do what was right for him, and if that meant giving him up, she was resigned to it. This was a real life Gift of the Magi story—the one where the husband sells his watch to buy his wife a comb for her long hair and the wife sells her hair to buy a watch fob for her husband. Like that story, this one, too, has a fairy tale ending. Tidy and Carole are great friends and are living together "happily ever after".

A(nother) True Fairy Tale

Once upon a time there was a promising puppy named Lou Lou. Everyone said she would "go far" in the conformation show ring. When she was old enough she went to her first dog show. She loved the atmosphere of the show scene; the excitement, the performing and she began to win. Every time she won, her handler and her person were thrilled and this made her happy and proud.

Then, all of a sudden, something changed. The important people in her life weren't having fun anymore. When she didn't win they became upset and sometimes even angry. Lou Lou didn't know what she was doing to cause this, but she began to dread going to shows. Where formerly she had pranced around the ring proudly, now she hung her head and looked dejected and...she didn't win.

Lou Lou's people had great plans for her. After her championship, they set their sights on the top prize: Number-One-Great-Dane-in-the-Nation, something never before accomplished by a dog of her sex and color. With this new goal came new pressures, however. Lou Lou had to win many shows to reach this goal, and to do this, she had to shine. Unfortunately, the people forgot to explain to Lou Lou that the goal was different and so were the requirements. As they became more ambitious and competitive, she became more overwhelmed.

As each show came and went and Lou Lou's demeanor cost her the win, the people became frantic. Time was slipping away and, with it, the top honors. At this point, they asked me to talk to her.

Lou Lou told me how much she loved her person and wanted to please her, but showing was no longer fun. She was overwhelmed by the responsibility of having to win and what she really wanted to do, now that her championship was behind her, was to go home and have babies to carry on her greatness.

My approach to trying to solve these problems and make everybody happy was multi-faceted. I explained to Lou Lou what her person's ambitions for her were. I explained Lou Lou's concerns to the people involved. I suggested a flower remedy for her, which included Elm for the overwhelming responsibility, Pine for self-reproach, and Wild Rose for resignation. The parties involved also made a deal. Lou Lou would make an effort to show this year and next year she would be bred.

The very next day, I watched her in the ring. The old attitude was back and she was "on". She won that day and many more until she did indeed finish the year as the Best in the Land.

Last week, which is nearly a year from my conversation with Lou Lou I got a "telepathic postcard" from her. She thanked me for helping her make her beloved person happy and to tell me she was pregnant.

Much happiness to you, Lou Lou, and may you and your puppies live happily ever after!

The Case of the "Autistic" Greyhound

The "sport" of racing Greyhounds leaves many casualties. They were virtually unseen until relatively recently when groups rescuing "retired" Greyhounds began to spring up. In New Hampshire alone, there are at least three groups I know of taking these dogs and finding loving, responsible homes for them.

In general, the dogs I've met are gentle, sweet, responsive and very grateful. Most seem to adapt very well into households, fitting in with children, dogs and other animals.

They come with a variety of challenges, however. Most have no hair on their hindquarters due, in part, to long hours spent in crates. For some, the hair grows back; for others, this physical scarring is permanent.

There are other scars, too, not initially as obvious. Such was the case with Lady, a five-year-old brindle (a color) female who had been with her person, Miriam, for a year.

During the foster home period, Lady seemed like a model citizen. Mechanically, she did everything she was asked to do. This made her a good candidate for adoption, and she went home with Miriam.

At her new home she wasn't rowdy and didn't chew household items. Then Miriam took her to obedience classes. Lady walked nicely at heel, but under no circumstances would she sit or lie down on request, nor would she come when called. She was still well behaved, but non-responsive.

Bonding between dog and human had begun, but didn't seem to progress. When Lady was at home, she spent most of her time hiding in the bedroom. Progress was so slow that Miriam was extremely frustrated. She had grown to love Lady, but wondered if she was truly reachable or if she had given her heart to yet another track casualty.

It was at this point that she brought Lady to me. At the beginning of our session, Miriam told me that she just wanted one indication that Lady might come to love her and respond to her. If she had that, she would have the strength to continue trying.

"Autistic" was the word that came to me as I sat and started talking telepathically to Lady. Yet, the more we talked, the more I realized that she had developed this withdrawn, protective, reclusive shell to protect herself from the rigors of the life she'd had to lead, but was not emotionally designed to handle. She had become a robot, a technique that actually had helped in several phases of her life. She loved to run, but she raced mechanically which caused her to be "retired". This robotic good behavior won her the term "adoptable" from her foster care guardians. Once she was adopted, however, the rules changed. Miriam wanted to be friends and partners and this Lady didn't know how to do.

While we talked, I used a form of energy healing on her developed by Linda Tellington-Jones called TTEAMwork. One of the underlying tenets of TTEAM is to use non-habitual movements to teach the cells new responses. The term "non-habitual" means something the dog doesn't expect. For example, dogs expect to be stroked when people touch them, but the circular TTEAM touches are unexpected. I decided to adapt this idea to hopefully change the relationship between Miriam and Lady. Rather than continuing on the unsuccessful road of traditional obedience training, I asked Miriam if there was any kind of music she particularly enjoyed listening to. Miriam replied that she especially liked Country and Western. I suggested that she put on music that she loved and then sit with Lady sharing the music and doing TTEAM (I taught her the basics) at the same time. The goal was to build on their stalled bonding process, develop trust and teach Lady how to respond emotionally. Once their relationship was on firmer ground, I felt Lady would be more responsive to traditional training.

Miriam's initial request to me had been to get something positive from our talk. Lady gave us not one, but two positive thoughts: 1) she was truly capable of responding and 2) she wanted to learn.

At the end of our session, she reached up and kissed me; it was then that I knew she would succeed.

Talking To Animals
Other Than Dogs and Cats

Most people who bring animals to me are focusing on their pets. But there are many other animals in the world, and it can be entertaining, even enlightening, and sometimes downright important to talk with them. When we lived in California, I taught a program which involved spending time at the zoo. Sometimes I would just sit on a bench and talk to the animals. During these times, I conversed with the giraffes, the lions, the wolves and the elephants, among others.

The giraffes were especially fun. The family unit consisted of a male, female, and baby. The male, particularly, was very shy, and would hide in the barn. After a few minutes of my talking to him mentally, he would peek around the corner to see who it was, and finally come all the way out to visit. It was fun to talk to these gentle creatures, and I, a novelty to them, helped to fill their days, too.

More recently, I had another experience talking to non-domesticated animals: a hungry group of yellow jackets. I had purchased chicken in bulk.

It was a lovely July day, and I hadn't given any thought to the hazards of leaving chicken packed in ice in the driveway for a few minutes until I could pack it up. When I got to it I discovered the yellow jackets had found a tasty feast for themselves!

I opened a box and threw a piece of chicken into the overturned lid. Then I concentrated on telling the insects that I had set aside a banquet just for them, if they would leave my portion alone. I worked as fast as I could, packaging my share, and wasn't bothered at all by the yellow jackets unless my concentration began to wander. Quickly, my mind would return to the business at hand. As soon as I asked them to leave mine alone, they did! I got my work done in record time, and left them to their feast.

You never know when it will come in handy to have a direct line of communication, regardless of the creature concerned!

Befriended by Phoebes

"Thank you for coming back to nest here, Phoebe," I said.

She replied, "You think I'm my mother, but I'm not. I was born here and remember it with safety."

I was excited. A second generation of phoebes at the same nest site. Thus began my five-week relationship with a most enjoyable bird and her four babies.

We had been impressed when the original phoebe built her nest here two years ago. She chose an excellent location, protected under the eaves of our garage. She built the nest high on top of a light, which came on at night. Not only did the warmth from the light take the chill off the night air, but also it attracted insects to her so she didn't even have to move to have a feast! The only disadvantage was that that she was next to the main door to our house. It didn't discourage her, though, and we did our best to minimize traffic by diverting everyone through the garage.

For three weeks, I occasionally kept her company as she sat on the nest. Sometimes we talked and other times just sat in companionable silence. Sometimes she left me in charge to "egg sit" while she was away for long periods hunting.

While Phoebe sat on the eggs, I asked her questions. I learned that she went "where the trees stay moist" in cold weather and that sitting on the nest was not boring, but a combination of vigilant awareness and a kind of trance-like meditative state. The trance helped her conserve energy in case she needed it, especially when she started feeding the babies.

I was surprised to find that a considerable amount of her activity was, indeed, instinctive. I've talked to so many animals and found that much of their behavior is well thought out. Therefore, it surprised me to verify that much of what the nature books say has some validity! For example, in answer to my query, "How do you know how to build your nest?" Her answer was, "I just do."

After three weeks, I asked her when the eggs would hatch and she told me to "look tomorrow." Sure enough, the next day the nest was filled with downy feathers attached to four hungry mouths! After that, there wasn't much time for conversation. The mother and father spent all the daylight hours bringing bugs for their voracious offspring. The parents were very cautious and spent long moments perched nearby, making sure it was safe, before flying up to the nest. The chicks were extremely quiet and I only heard little peeps at the moment of food delivery.

I was astonished at how quickly they grew. They grew from hatchlings to fledglings in fewer than two weeks! Soon the chicks were so big that they had to sit on each other to fit into the tiny nest.

There was quite a bit of preparation prior to fledging. New feathers replaced the down they were born with and the stiff casing surrounding the feathers had to be removed. Lots of preening took place as they helped each other by preening in those hard-to-reach places.

The final step was wing exercise. Two at a time they started flapping their wings while balancing on the edge of the nest. As they got stronger they began to lift and it looked as though they were levitating! All through the fledging day, the parents fed them and then put on displays to encourage the chicks to follow them.

One brave soul took the plunge and launched himself to a nearby bush. After resting and more preening (and posing for some pictures!) he managed to fly to a tree and then to the roof. Soon, he was zipping around like a pro!

The others took longer, preening, resting and levitating, but suddenly, after hours of delay, they too were gone.

"Thanks for sharing your lives with us, phoebes," I called to them mentally. "Come again."

After those five intense weeks the nest quickly became covered with cobwebs like the abandoned house that it was. I went inside to call the driveway man to do the work we'd had to delay for my wild bird lesson.

Lost, But Often Not Found

"My dog/cat/bird is lost," the caller starts out. "Can you help me?"

I love my job as an animal communicator, but of the many types of calls I get, this one always makes my heart sink. Some animal communicators feel so strongly about lost animal calls that they refuse to do them at all.

"Why?" you ask. "Isn't this the pinnacle of being an animal communicator? Just ask the animal where she is and she can say, "I'm at the corner of Hollywood and Vine wearing a red beret. Come and get me!"

Oh! I wish it were something like that. The fact is, something happens to animals when they're lost. Their perceptions change and the information I get from them is often unreliable.

Sometimes animals don't know if they're alive or dead so the ensuing communication I receive from them feels the same to me either way. Unless the death has been a traumatic one, they may not mention it, may not even know when you ask them and/or can't tell.

A Whippet named J.B. slipped out of a boarding kennel while his people were on vacation. By the time they called me, he'd been lost for two weeks. During the next week, I was able to tune into him and he gave me many landmarks, which his people were able to confirm. We tracked him for about five miles and there were several sightings in one neighborhood. J. B. was in what I call "survival mode" when I first tuned in to him and remained in that state for a long time.

Suddenly, one day, I felt an energy shift as though he'd made some sort of breakthrough. His focus shifted from survival to his family, and he told me he was coming home. Unfortunately, he didn't tell me what caused this change of focus. It turned out that some people had found him the day before who had taken him to the veterinarian. The veterinarian thought him beyond repair so he was euthanized. Once J.B. was released from his physical body and the challenges it brought him, he was able to function well again. This allowed him to think about his family, but for them, of course, it was not to be the same.

Animals sometimes tell me where they wish they were, rather than where they actually are. Beth, a German Shepherd/Collie mix, was trapped in the foundation of a new house where she was eventually found. She passed her day thinking about a farm she visited regularly. Her person verified that she often went to a farm fitting the description I saw and had to be retrieved from there frequently. Obviously, I was talking to the right dog, but she wouldn't answer my question, "Where are you now?" Instead, she shared her thoughts about where she wanted to be.

When lost animals go into survival mode, they find it hard to concentrate on their former domestic lives; all their energy goes into being safe and finding food and water. They often share this information with me, but it doesn't get us any closer to reunion. They go into a twilight zone where all humans represent a threat, so that even when their people are close by calling them, they concentrate on their safety. They truly revert, in a fundamental way, to their wild instincts.

The biggest benefit of working with an animal communicator is that I rarely have difficulty tuning in telepathically because they are employing communication skills used in the wild. This sometimes helps to bump them out of this "survival twilight zone" to start relating to people again. Obviously, this was happening with J.B. as he finally went to a person for help. If I can talk lost animals into approaching people, their chances of being found and returned increase.

There have been some rewarding successes among my lost animal searches, however.

Hokey, a Siamese cat lives in a big city where his person allows him and his housemate to play on the fire escape. From there they go to the roof to play. Sometimes they are allowed to play in the apartment building hallway instead. One day, the other cat returned, but Hokey didn't and his person wasn't sure which direction to look. Hokey told me he had gone through a door and was outside on the street! He had gone back inside with another person but he didn't think he was in the right building.

With that information, his person abandoned her search of the roof and put flyers in adjacent buildings instead. Sure enough, someone spotted him and called her. This was a happy reunion!

This story is heartwarming and is what keeps me from the ranks of those refusing lost animal calls entirely, but it is unfortunately not the norm. The most secure animals sometimes find themselves in unusual situations and often they change from gregarious animals who are confident around people, to cautious individuals who hide from all humans. In this type of circumstance, the success rate of recovery is very low.

It goes without saying that we always need to be concerned with security where our animal companions are concerned. Identification tattooing is also strongly recommended. Tattooing allows animals to "phone home" when found. Not being lost in the first place is ideal, however. Please be aware and vigilant. Hopefully, I'll not be receiving any "help, my animal is lost" call from you!

Betty Lewis, RVT, Dr. A.N.

VERNE

Chapter II

Animals Speak! About Telepathy for Healing

One of the most useful areas for telepathic communication is in the area of health.

"If only the animals could tell us where it hurts!" I've said it myself and so has every veterinarian I worked for when I was an active veterinary technician. It's *so* frustrating to know an animal is in pain and not be able to identify the problem. Even we humans can have a difficult time, sometimes, being able to tell our doctor where or how it hurts. Of course, even with telepathy, the animal won't be able to say "I have pancreatitis." or "I have a foxtail in my ear," but she *can* say "I have a sharp pain in my abdomen," or "There's something sticking me in the ear".

Animals communicate through a variety of techniques. Sometimes I "just know" what's the matter; sometimes I feel the pain in the corresponding area in my own body. Sometimes I can "see" the problem in my mind's eye, such as a red, irritated area. However the message comes, it's important to follow through. The outcome can be the relief of pain or the changing of a life story.

Drummer- a*Great* Great Dane

Champion Waccabuc's Different Drummer was one of my own Great Danes.

He was a tall, easy going, fun loving, brindle (refers to his color: fawn with black stripes) boy who never failed to be waiting at the door when I returned from being away. He was always grinning and wagging his tail, a greeting which uplifted me every time I came home.

This particular day, the Wednesday before Thanksgiving, I got home from work about an hour after my son, Brian. As he

17

did every day, Brian had let the dogs out when he came home from school and then back in again when they were ready. Drummer was at the door as usual when I arrived, but nothing else was the same. Instead of the ears-up, tail-wagging dog who generally greeted me, Drum's head was down, his back was hunched in pain, and his tail, though still wagging, was held tightly between his legs. His posture was bad enough, but what *really* scared me was that he could only walk in a straight line. If he tried to turn, as he walked around the kitchen, he fell over. This was a dog who had been totally normal and sound only hours earlier. Now he looked like the end stage of some severe degenerative neurological disease.

"My God, what happened to you?" I cried. Immediately he answered, telepathically, and, a moving picture began in my head. I clearly saw Drummer running in our hilly, wooded back yard where wet leaves covered the ground. Suddenly, he lost his footing. His left hind leg went underneath him and he fell, hard, on his left side, hitting his head against a tree as he landed.

Now I knew *how* he had injured himself. I didn't know what his injuries were, but I knew what avenue to take to help Drummer to recovery. I suspected torn or bruised muscles, not something that could be helped by a conventional veterinarian. However, had I not had the input from Drum's own story, I would have set off blindly to a veterinarian. He probably would have taken x-rays that would have been inconclusive. Cage rest would have been the probable advice and I would have ended up with a compromised dog in chronic pain.

Instead, I called our chiropractor who saw Drummer after his office hours. All creatures are subject to the conditions which chiropractors can help and dogs are no exception.

Drummer was adjusted at 9:30 that Wednesday night. He rested all day Thanksgiving and missed dog shows on Friday and Saturday. Sunday, however, while not quite as good as new, he was sound enough to be shown. He fully recovered and easily finished his championship after that. What a happy ending to a story which so easily could have gone the other way.

Ginger- a Welsh Pony

Ginger itched all over and was rubbing her hair off by scratching on anything available: walls, fences, even people! Ginger's people suspected that black flies, which plague us during the spring in New England, might be the culprit.

Ginger was in a nice corral when I got to her home, but she was certainly a scruffy looking being.

I started by asking her about the bugs and if she was bothered by the flies. To our surprise, she said the flies didn't really bother her that much.   After further investigatory questions, it turned out that well-meaning though they were, her people were not providing adequate nutrition. Ginger was shedding, a normal event which can cause itching in and of itself, but due to her diet, she was deficient in nutrients needed to keep her skin moist and encourage the regrowth of her coat. Once dietary changes were made, Ginger's hair grew in normally and the itching stopped.

Sweet Dreams- a Thoroughbred

Sweet Dreams was a 12 year old Thoroughbred, living in a private barn in New York not far from Donna's apartment. Donna, his person, called me in a panic. Her regular communicator was out of town, could I help?

Sweetie had been confined to his stall for the past year due to a ligament injury. His injury had finally healed and Sweetie had been outside cavorting and celebrating his new found freedom when he suddenly became lame. Donna was desperate to know what had happened: was this the old injury or something else?

Animals are often better tuned into their own bodies than we seem to be, but Sweetie is extraordinarily aware. He was able to describe his injury to me. He told me the location and showed me what appeared to be a frayed rope. A torn flexor tendon turned out to be the veterinary diagnosis.

Sweetie and Donna were understandably devastated by the thought of another year that would be wasted in confinement. Depression and despondence threatened to take all their energy.

For emotional support, to get through this new ordeal, Sweetie and I worked out some Bach Flower Essences for him to use. Flower essences are gentle energy which stabilize emotions. Elm for being overwhelmed, gorse for hopelessness and olive for exhaustion, helped him to get through the initial shock. We also worked out some nutritional and herbal changes to his established protocol, but most important was my recommendation to find a holistic practitioner who could help Sweetie to heal on a deep level.

A series of calls from Donna to me followed. Two veterinarians and a holistic body worker had recommended euthanasia. This was disheartening but Sweetie maintained that he wasn't on his way out yet! Finally, after many calls and some dead end leads, Donna found a rehabilitation barn in Pennsylvania where she could move Sweetie.

The move was a difficult choice to make. It was out of state, so Donna could only see Sweetie on weekends rather than every night, and she and Sweetie missed each other terribly. However it was the right move to make because Sweetie would get the care he needed from the gifted resident veterinarian and dedicated staff.

Under the intensive hands-on care Sweetie received at the rehabilitation barn, coupled with continuous feedback from Sweetie himself, he began to heal. Within two months of the initial call, Sweetie was sound, and back outside enjoying the fresh air and sunshine.

Donna is back to riding Sweet Dreams on the weekends when she visits and there's even been talk of him being shown in the future. Without Donna's perseverance, Sweetie's intimate knowledge of himself, my being able to interpret Sweetie's information and the expertise of the medical staff, Sweetie wouldn't have had a chance to live a normal life. The ability of all of us to work together has given him that opportunity.

And, after less than two years of rehabilitation and preparation, Sweetie competed in his first show, soundly taking 24 jumps!

Sheba- a Great Dane Rescue

Sometimes people bring dogs into their families and the relationship doesn't work out for one reason or another. For this reason, rescue organizations for the different breeds have sprung up around the country. This is a good system for several reasons: people who are dedicated to certain breeds can work actively to make sure the breed they love is adequately cared for. People who are looking for a certain breed can contact a specific rescue organization and have a greater chance of finding a dog who will be compatible. The dogs, caught in the middle through no fault of their own, find a second chance at a good life.

Sheba was a Rescue, a harlequin Great Dane who got a second chance with her new person, Michele. Sheba's mission was short, but the lessons she taught were profound.

When Sheba came into her life, Michele found and joined the Great Dane Mailing List on the Internet to learn as much about Great Danes as possible. (See Appendix III "Resources" for more information.) One of the many things Michele learned was how much healthier it is for dogs to eat a raw, natural diet, rather than processed food. Sheba was gradually switched to an all raw diet, a move which was to help tremendously during the ordeal which was to follow.

One day, about two and a half years after Sheba joined her family Michele e-mailed me saying that Sheba was sick. The first indication that something was wrong was that Sheba began to drink and urinate more than usual. A blood test revealed abnormal liver enzymes. Shortly after this, she also began to retain fluid, and then the veterinary diagnosis came indicating advanced cirrhosis of the liver.

At this point, Sheba, Michele and I began to have regular communications. Sheba showed me that she was having a toxic reaction. Michele did some detective work to try to discover how Sheba had managed to get so sick. She wrote some of her conclusions this way:

"She eats grass just about everywhere! Remember, we walk twice a day up to about a mile and it's all manicured lawns that we walk by here in the suburbs. When she's walking, she looks like a Bloodhound, with her nose constantly to the ground 'reading the news', and snarfing up grass." It seemed fairly certain that Sheba had become toxic on lawn pesticides and herbicides from the highly treated grass.

Fortunately, Michele and her husband were in the process of fencing their yard so Sheba would have her own place to play and not have to rely on walks for exercise. At least the ingestion of *more* toxic grass was about to come to an end. The question was, could we detoxify Sheba, and was the damage already done to her liver reversible?

Despite adding liver-supportive herbs and cleansing foods and juices, Sheba's condition worsened. However, during the course of her illness, she had many good days. She reveled in the freedom of her new fenced yard, and sometimes played fairly energetically with her housemate, a little dog named Casey.

More lessons were to come as Michele consulted a holistic veterinarian and learned about homeopathy and acupuncture. With each visit, Sheba rallied a little, but not enough to be considered "recovering". Finally, after about three months of trying many treatments, she told me that she wanted Michele to know that recovery was not really likely. She already had a compromised liver when she came into Michele's life due to poor care and especially poor water in her previous home. She wanted Michele to know this and to realize that it wasn't her fault.

In the end, Sheba didn't survive the toxic insult to her body. However, she had had three extra months with her family and many good days. During the course of her illness, she had taught Michele some very valuable lessons. Shortly after her release from her compromised body, she sent Jake, a merle Great Dane, another Rescue, to enjoy the fruits of the seeds she had sown.

Jake is on a natural diet, has two caring veterinarians (one allopath, one holistic) and honors Sheba as he runs around her safe back yard. He is bringing joy into the lives of his humans and living a healthier, happier life thanks to the lessons Sheba taught so eloquently.

Phyllis- a cat with a growth

The first time I worked with Phyllis, an 8 year old black cat, she appeared to be perfectly normal, although a bit thin. The appointment had actually been for a companion cat who was very sick. After working with Blackjack, Carrie asked if I'd give Phyllis a Therapeutic Touch (TT) treatment so she wouldn't feel left out.

When I started working with Phyllis, I thought it was going to be a routine, healthy cat energy "tune up", but I felt an area on her chest which seem "congested". I didn't actually understand the implications at the time, but we noted the energy imbalance.

Two months later Carrie was back in my office with Phyllis who now had a golf-ball sized lump just below her sternum. The veterinarian diagnosed her with cancer, but hadn't offered much in the way of allopathic choices. He felt the lump was too well attached to perform a safe surgery. Carrie declined chemotherapy.

I suggested to Carrie that she increase the raw foods that Phyllis had available, to increase the Super Blue Green Algae she was already taking and to use Essiac tea, an herbal blend which has been helpful to others when dealing with situations such as this.

Over the next few weeks, I saw Phyllis several times and did TT on her each time. By about the third session, I was having difficulty finding the lump and the last time I saw her, I couldn't find it at all. Phyllis went on to gain her weight back and is back to total health.

Mabel and Callie

Mabel came to me because she was concerned about her cats. She had recently acquired a young second cat, and the first one was having a difficult time adjusting.

The twelve year-old, Callie, had stopped eating and wasn't grooming, but a veterinary exam revealed nothing wrong. The cats had occasional half-hearted spats, but otherwise ignored each other since they had separate eating areas. Callie's downhill spiral was worrisome, and Mabel was beginning to despair of their being "one big happy family".

I entered the picture at that point, and talked to the cats. Callie told me that, in actuality, the two of them had worked out everything between them already. However, she was having a lot of fun keeping the household in turmoil. Manipulation of the situation was giving her a feeling of power, and I got the distinct feeling that she said to me, "Just look what disruption a twelve year-old lady can achieve!"

Further investigation revealed that the cats played and got along fine when Mabel wasn't home, but Callie put on an act as soon as she arrived. Treatment of this situation was as follows:

First, I told Callie that "the jig was up!" Now that her person knew what was going on, there would be no need to continue her behavior. Secondly, both cat and human took appropriate Bach Flower Remedies to balance their emotional patterns. A second person in the household was to give extra attention to the new cat and Mabel would pay special attention to Callie.

Two weeks later I heard from them again. Both cats were sleeping in the bedroom and eating from dishes side-by-side. They didn't yet play together in front of my Mabel, but had given up their little fights. Callie was again grooming herself and was contented. Life was back to normal.

Karen and Joanne

Every year The Great Dane Club of America holds its National Specialty Show in a different location. 1992 found me flying to San Antonio, Texas where I would visit with old friends and make some new ones. But this year had an added dimension which made this trip particularly special.

Two days before I left, I received a call from a wildlife rehabilitator in San Antonio, who wanted to know how she could help a seven week old squirrel she had named Joanne. Joanne had been pushed from her nest and was having difficulty recovering from the trauma. I agreed to come to her home and work with Joanne. This worked perfectly for me, too, as I needed a ride from the airport to the dog show.

The first time I worked with Joanne, I focussed mainly on her physical body. She had been badly bruised in the fall and had swollen hock (ankle) joints. I did energy work on her including Therapeutic Touch and TTEAMwork. It was a treat for me to hold this little being. I fed her apples and grapes and taught her to eat a pecan!

The second time we worked together, two days later, she had improved quite a bit. The swelling had receded, hair was growing back on her legs, and she was starting to chatter. She was beginning to hold her tail up, something she hadn't done two days before, and she was trying to stand on her hind legs to eat pecans. The physical improvements were gratifying, but more exciting was her willingness to talk to me. In the course of my experience in talking with animals, I have talked with a few squirrels, but rarely have I had an opportunity to do so on such a personal basis!

One improvement Joanne hadn't yet made was to hold her ears up in characteristic squirrel fashion. When I asked her about this, she seemed surprised to find out that she had ears! While doing TTEAM on her ears to bring her awareness to that part of her body and to stimulate her acupuncture points, I discussed the function of ears and importance they would have when she was released. Within moments, she was using her ears!

25

I learned that Joanne seemed to work in slow motion. Knowing this allowed me to suggest to the rehabilitator that Joanne would need some special introductions to events which would most likely be in her environment later. I felt that if she had special preparation now, she would have a better chance for survival.

On a larger scale, it was clear Joanne was sent as a teacher. By observing a squirrel's growth and development in "slow motion," Karen would have better understanding of the needs of other orphaned squirrels.

Bach Flower Remedies

I have been asked whether Bach Flower Remedies can be used in healing animals as they are in healing people, and the answer is a resounding "yes!" Sometimes they work better and faster with animals than with people because animals have no preconceived notions that get in the way!

Rescue Remedy is so important that I always carry a vial in my purse. I've used it for dogs who have become frightened in crowds or other similar situations. I use it for my male dogs when my bitches are in season, and they cease the characteristic panting, whining and pacing they tend to do during that time. I even used it once to resuscitate a dog who had been inadvertently strangled to death by a tight collar. Cardiac massage brought back the heartbeat and Rescue Remedy brought back respiration.

Animals' emotions are the same as ours, so aspen is excellent for the easily intimidated cat who hides under the bed when strangers come into the house. Mimulus can help dogs who are afraid of thunder or other loud noises such as firecrackers on the Fourth of July. Honeysuckle is useful to help an animal work through grief when a family member (animal or human) has died. Chicory can help ease "separation anxiety" for the dog who becomes upset when you are gone and becomes destructive in the house.

A woman came to me because one of her cats was spraying in the house. This cat was pretty cavalier about the whole thing and didn't take the consequences of his behavior too seriously. Offering a few flimsy excuses, he confessed that he sprayed because he felt like it, since he wanted to be the boss. He had decided that this was the most effective means to get his way. I made several suggestions to the person for changing his behavior and had a serious talk with the cat. Then, to help him cope with new restrictions and to ease his transition to a different behavior, I suggested she give him Rescue Remedy with vine and cherry plum. The cherry plum helped him to take control of himself and vine to balance his tendencies to become a dictator. Within a week, the household was back to normal.

Of course it is always important to talk to your animals and find out why they are behaving as they are. Then, in conjunction with appropriate therapy, Bach Flowers are a tremendous support.

Gloria, an Eastern Box Turtle

Sometimes talking to animals can clarify physical problems and facilitate treatment. Gloria, an Eastern Box Turtle, had been rescued while crossing a busy highway. She remained with her rescuer, visiting for ten months and living in a terrarium.

During December of the second winter, Gloria began having some physical problems, and the one of greatest concern was that she stopped eating. A veterinarian was consulted and Gloria was placed on antibiotics. The owner was cautioned: "Do not let her hibernate."

Accordingly, the heat was kept up in Gloria's terrarium. But after five weeks of not eating, and no apparent improvement from veterinary care, the owner called me.

I used several alternative healing modalities with Gloria, including chakra balancing, Therapeutic Touch, and TTEAM work (a touch technique developed by Linda Tellington-Jones specifically for animals.) We also prepared a Bach Flower

Remedy. Gloria was given a Vitalite (a full spectrum artificial light) and purified water.

Most importantly, however, Gloria and I chatted. She was most personable and curious, and loved to be stroked. I took to her right away. My strong feeling was that despite the summer-like heat and light in her living area, Gloria's biological clock was at "high hibernation," and she was otherwise healthy. She did say that "food that moved" would be welcome. I also got feelings that she was preparing to be mated but, in the absence of a mate, she wasn't too clear what to do about that.

After a nearly disastrous trip to yet another veterinarian—where they inadvertently ruptured the egg she had been incubating —all medications were discontinued. Gloria began to respond to the addition of "mealie worms" to her diet (food that moved), and to some of the holistic techniques I taught the owner to use at home. Within a few weeks, Gloria recovered uneventfully.

"There's no substitute for talking to the patient." - Norman Cousins

Norman Cousins was referring to human patients, of course, when he made the above statement. He was criticizing physicians for treating ill people the way we, of necessity, generally treat animals. However, talking to the animal and finding out what is really going on can be critical to the accuracy of the diagnosis and success of treatment.

A Lhasa Apso, Heidi, was brought to me after two years of treatment by veterinarians. The original complaint was that she had urine accidents in the house. The initial diagnosis was cystitis and the dog was put on what is considered appropriate medications for this condition. Over the course of the two years, many inconclusive tests were run, different medications were tried but nothing really seemed to have a lasting effect. Veterinary care was escalated. Heidi and her person were referred to other veterinarians including the School of Veterinary

Medicine at Tufts University. Finally, they were told that there was only one highly sophisticated test that would give them the answer. It was performed only a few times yearly at another university! At that point, Heidi's person re-evaluated the strategy entirely and called me.

In our initial visit I simply talked to the dog and asked, "Why do you urinate in the house?" She responded that she was the boss and bosses are allowed to do whatever they want to! It sounded like sound reasoning to me! The problem was identified as easily as that. From then on we could address and solve the correct problem. I presented several suggestions and, by the next visit, Heidi was only "stating" her feeling of superiority every few days rather than several times a day. Over the course of several months other dominance related problems surfaced as the dog and person readjusted their roles. So much unnecessary expense, aggravation, and chemical assault on the body could have been avoided if only someone had initially been able to talk to the patient.

Another case of inappropriate elimination involved an otherwise delightful and affectionate cat who was spraying in the house. He told me how he just couldn't seem to control himself. There was a female in the neighborhood who was in season and, try as he might, he was unable to control his natural inclinations. I sent his person home with several courses of action, and the problem was resolved.

When I called to find out how the cat was doing, I found that the problem had come back. Again, we visited, but this time a very different cat persona emerged. This time, the cat had made a conscious decision to spray as a way of getting attention. He was quite resentful of my trying to change his behavior and showed it by hiding in a corner. He did, however, cooperate with our discussion and gave me several useful insights into why he needed more attention and what steps could be taken to shift his behavior from something intolerable to humans to something everyone could live with.

Often considerable dedication to solving the problem is required by the humans involved, but I know that we would have had NO chance to be successful if we had simply tried to use the same techniques that had worked before. "There's no substitute for talking to the patient."

The Betty Theory of Disease

People call me to talk to their animals for a variety of reasons. Some are just curious about what their animals have to say and if they are happy in their present circumstances. One lady gave a visit to me as a present to her dog for the dog's birthday! Shadow and I had a nice conversation (shared with her person, of course!) and Shadow had a relaxing TTEAM (Tellington-Jones technique) experience.

However, most people call because things are not right, and the overwhelming number come because of health-related issues, either physical or emotional.

This has led me to ponder the similarities that link them together and for lack of a better term, I am calling this The Betty Theory of Disease.

Underlying the specific issues or symptoms which manifest in each individual is what our society has labeled "stress."

One theory of stress says that every event in life has a **stress score**. There are no positives or negatives, just a score. So, marriage and divorce, birth and death, all have **stress scores** and they are cumulative at any time in our lives.

Second, we each have a **stress threshold**. That is, through various coping techniques and the nature of ourselves, there's a level of stress which doesn't bother us particularly.

Third, something may occur that causes our cumulative stress score to bump over the stress threshold. When that happens, the theory says, you will have a health change. That is, the cumulative stress above the coping level is more than the body can handle and the immune system develops a crack somewhere to let in some kind of "bug."

If you accept that, it comes as no surprise that we, and our animals may become ill as a response to events, small and large, which all lead to a **stress fracture**!

Another way to look at this is an analogy I frequently use. Picture an empty glass. Into the glass you add drops of water, one at a time. Each drop represents a stress, which can be emotional, physical or spiritual imbalance and often comes in the form of environmental toxins. Drop by drop, the glass begins to fill up. In goes a drop for both humans spending long hours at work while their animal companion is home alone all day. Another drop represents tap water, another is commercial pet food, others might be vaccinations, a family member's illness, traffic exhaust in the street, the neighbor's decision to use a chemical lawn company, a colicky baby who cries in distress, a cold floor, a hot day, lack of exercise, too much exercise, and on and on and on.

All these drops go into the glass and if no drops are ever removed, eventually the glass becomes full and then spills over. At this point, a health crisis occurs. This is when we see symptoms and become alarmed. We may even say the problem developed "suddenly", when, in fact, as you can see, it was really developing over some period of time.

Our job, then, is to be aware of the drops going in and to try to limit them, while at the same time, looking for ways to take drops out.

Three areas that I target with the majority of my clients are pure water, environmental toxins and diet. If you do nothing but address these areas, you may be able to raise the thresholds so dramatically that you never see any symptoms indicating an overflowing glass.

Water is the number one nutrient, after oxygen, required by our bodies. Bodies are reported to be about 75% water. Therefore, it is important to provide the best quality. Quality water used to be something we could take for granted, but no more! Municipal sources are often polluted, and then sanitized by using the toxic chemical chlorine. People say to me, "but I have well water!" as though not knowing the source of our water somehow makes it better! Are you certain that underground aquifer is pristine? Are you downhill from your neighbor's septic system? The only thing better about well water is that no chlorine or fluoride has been added. Beyond that, we don't really know what's in it and the standard water analysis which proclaims our water "safe" doesn't begin to test of the number of possible contaminants.

The only way we can be sure our water is pure is by purifying it ourselves. Water purifiers come in a variety of categories from small countertop models to whole house units. My information says that the best kind is a reverse osmosis unit. Don't be fooled into thinking that a carbon filter on the faucet is enough. Bottled water from the grocery store may be an expedient compromise in the short-term, either during the transition to a home purifier or while traveling, but this industry is little regulated and you could be drinking someone else's tap water!

Incidentally, water is also known as the universal solvent, which means that it has the ability to dissolve materials and incorporate them into itself. That plastic water dish you let water sit in all day is a toxic waste dump! Use only stainless steel or glass for your animal's food and water dishes, please!

I am harping on this topic because water quality is such a critical issue and we have been lulled for so many years to believe in the safety of our water supply. We find it easy to just ignore this part, believing that it doesn't pertain to us. For your own health and that of your animals, do something about your water quality today.

The second area where we unwittingly bombard our animals with toxins is in the very act of trying to make things safe for them: chemicals used in the environment. This is a big topic and it ranges from cleaning products to insect repellants. Do you use any products ending in -sol to clean your home? These are among the most toxic to animals! There is an excellent book by Nina Anderson and Howard Peiper called *Are You Poisoning*

Your Pets? Many cleaning jobs can be effectively completed by using baking soda, vinegar and lemon juice. Environmentally friendly and non-toxic cleaning supplies can also be obtained commercially. This book gives you many alternatives to toxic cleaning supplies.

Other environmental toxins can include over-vaccination (see Appendix I.) Do you walk your dog? If so, be very wary of manicured lawns. Pretty to look at, but hazardous to live near. (Remember Michele and Sheba?) I know of a dog whose foot-pads sloughed off after one exposure to lawn chemicals at a motel. He was a great stud dog who was also rendered sterile for many months following this incident.

Cats are even more sensitive than dogs, yet they get to roam free— free to be exposed without our even knowing it!

Especially in northern climates, where our houses are practically air-tight during the winter, our air quality may be compromised. Maybe this is the year to investigate an air filter, or better yet, an ozonator. This machine ionizes the air allowing dust and microbes to settle where they can be mechanically removed. Simultaneously the air is oxygenated.. Recently, I've read alarming statistics about the declining percentage of oxygen in our atmosphere. With this type of machine, you can add some of it back, at least indoors.

The final area which you can change to have a serious positive health impact on your animals is in the area of diet. This topic is monumental, the subject of many books. There are excellent resources to help you to transition your animals to a species appropriate raw diet. There are several basic books and the Internet has wonderful support and the experiences of people feeding the recently re-discovered old way of feeding naturally.

In general, these books detail how we have been led astray and even duped by the multi-million dollar pet food industry and how you can sensibly, safely and economically provide a quality home-made diet for your pets. There is too much information to even summarize it here, but this one change in an animal's life has been known to reverse the downhill slide and add quality years to the lives of many animals.

This happened recently in a very dramatic way to a black Great Dane named Bennie. His veterinarian made the initial contact with me because he'd "tried everything" and was at his wit's end. Bennie chewed at his feet constantly to the point where his toes were facing amputation if his self-mutilation couldn't be stopped. The dog had a nice personality. The family loved him and the hospital staff was attached to him, but the very real threat of euthanasia loomed in his future.

The family made an appointment and brought Bennie to see me. I will not describe what I saw, but it was not a pretty sight.

Within a few minutes of talking with Bennie, I realized that he was telling me that he was literally starving and was cannibalizing himself for food. He was definitely a very thin dog, but he ate 10 cups of a commercial dog food daily. His veterinarians had told the people that a thin dog was healthier than an obese one, so they figured they were doing okay.

Our consultation then focused on diet. I sent them home with several recommendations, including a raw diet and natural whole food supplements, and asked them to call me in three weeks after they'd had a chance to implement my suggestions.

A few weeks went by and I didn't hear from them. A few more weeks elapsed and I tried to reach them. Finally, after two months, I got through. I was convinced that the reason they hadn't called was that they had put him down and were afraid to tell me. Therefore, I was ecstatic to find that not only was Bennie alive, but he was doing well! He was filling out and happy and playful. He still licked his feet—maybe out of habit- but they were healing. The whole family had pulled together and were united in their commitment to Bennie's recovery. Joyful news! and ...a credit to the power of good food!

Stress, an innocuous, almost meaningless word. It's been said that without stress, we'd all be dead. Therefore, the goal isn't to eliminate it, but to regulate, and modify it. We need to recognize that stress is a part of life and we must be always vigilant in finding ways to take some of those toxic drops out of the glass so that the unavoidable ones we must live with won't have a devastating impact.

Addressing these three issues can insure that you will have your animals with you for a long time to fulfill their highest potentials.

Chapter III

Animals Speak! About Behavior

Animal behaviorists usually rely on their knowledge of "normal" behavior in animals when trying to solve conflicts between people and their animals. Then, they compare the presenting behavioral challenge with the normal behavior, and through trial and error attempt to resolve the problem. This often works, but it basically relies on educated guessing.

I've found that talking to the animals themselves and asking what's wrong often shortcuts the process. Sometimes, no, *often* just making the appointment with me changes the animal's behavior, indicating that they only wanted to be heard!

The following stories illustrate some behavior conflicts, which were resolved by talking to the animals and asking them for their side of the story.

Snorkel

Snorkel was a five year old Miniature Longhaired Dachshund. He had been housebroken for all of his five years, but suddenly began to lift his leg in the house. His family was having difficulty coping with this new behavior and asked me what was going on.

At the time, the family was on an emotional roller coaster. The two children were teenagers (difficult enough, as those of us who have had teenaged children know) and there were other challenges being faced as well. It might be logical to assume that Snorkel was making a statement or responding to the heightened emotional climate in the home. However, when I asked him, "Why are you suddenly urinating in the house," his answer had nothing to do with the people. He told me that he was now the Boss Dog and this was what you had to do, right? I asked my client what this could mean and she said that their older dog had recently been diagnosed with prostate cancer and, as a result, had been neutered. This, indeed, changed the status of the two dogs.

Snorkel's leg lifting days rapidly ceased after I explained to him it wasn't actually necessary. He really never wanted the job of Boss Dog anyway and was quite relieved to go back to being himself. After a few more experimental marking episodes, he stopped entirely.

Rumpelstiltskin & Chris

The first time Rumpelstiltskin came to see me he was a big, bold, macho cat. He walked into my office exuding self-reliance, strutting about, investigating things, rubbing on me and the furniture and generally making the place his own. His person, Chris complained that he had started to spray in the house, but Rumpelstiltskin was unconcerned. He brushed off our attempts to discuss the situation with casual excuses.

"Oh, there's an animal in season outside," he said. "I guess I can't help it; I'm just a cat!" Another comment was "Maybe I'm not the one doing it." His remarks were unconvincing to me, but he didn't take it seriously enough for us to enlist his cooperation in stopping.

Therefore, my suggestion to Chris was to place the responsibility for stopping this behavior squarely on his shoulders. She was to get a crate, which was large enough to be a comfortable residence. It was to be large enough to contain a litter box as well as sleeping quarters and he was confined to it when not being directly supervised. The plan was not to punish the cat by locking him up, but to provide an alternative lifestyle, which was acceptable to all sides. Rumpelstiltskin was to earn "free time" privileges by ceasing to spray when he was loose in the house.

After two days of the new arrangement, he decided to quit the spraying entirely and the household returned to normal.

This isn't the end of the story, however. I was writing an article and wanted to use his story as an example, so I called to find out how he was doing. I was told that all had been well for about 9 months, but recently Rumpelstiltskin had started to spray again.

When Rumpelstiltskin arrived at my office this time, I didn't recognize him as the same cat. Gone were the highly confident attitude and the "devil may care" approach. Instead, he found the "hiding shelf" where insecure cats often hang out and we had our chat with him hidden from my view.

"I don't think she loves me anymore," he confessed. She's gone long hours and sometimes has someone else come and take care of me.

Upon questioning, it came out that Chris was being laid off from her job. The company had offered her the option of another position within the company, but it required that she spend extra hours doing computer searches for job openings and then follow up in person by travelling to check out the possibilities in person.

Confinement to a crate would certainly have been the wrong approach to take under these circumstances. In fact, it likely would have made the situation worse, possibly leading to enough stress to cause him to block his urinary tract, a life-threatening situation for a cat.

Instead, we explained the situation and made it very clear that Chris wasn't ignoring him, but had some lifestyle changes to consider and was trying to find the best situation for them both. In addition, when she *was* home, she was to make a special effort to spend quality time with Rumpelstiltskin.

Further, there were the Bathroom Conversations. This is a technique I devised for people who must spend time away from their animals.

It starts at home. Put pictures of your animals, or even just sticky notes with their names on them, in your bathroom. Condition yourself that every time you go into that room, you think about your animals. When this becomes an automatic habit, you can take the behavior with you when you travel. Since no one questions what you're doing when you're using a bathroom, you can afford a few extra private minutes to think about and talk to the animals at home. Just concentrate on them, tell them you love them and that you'll be home in however many days are remaining. Once the animals realize you're checking in at intervals during the day, they're often waiting for your "call". Try it, you may be amazed at what happens!

This approach was just what Rumelstiltskin needed. He literally bounded out of the hiding shelf and jumped into Chris' lap. Subsequently, they both moved to Chicago where they are both much happier.

Sarah

"Sarah's acting very oddly," the caller said. "It started about two weeks ago with her 'hovering' near me every moment. She won't let me out of her sight! If I ask her if she wants to go outside, she slinks away as though she were being punished! And another thing, she's broken her housebreaking and is using the dining room as her bathroom. Something is terribly wrong here."

Sarah turned out to be a two and a half year old Great Dane who had been adopted at five weeks — far too young to leave a litter, but obviously circumstances beyond her control dictated this poor start in life! By the age of two, she'd already borne two litters, and the circumstances surrounding the second litter had been a horrendous experience for the young dog. She had been sent away — "rented out" — to an unfamiliar household in Texas to give birth. Sarah's person said the woman in Texas had been reluctant to return her after the puppies were gone.

When Sarah did return home, she discovered that one of her canine companions had died in her absence. Nevertheless, she seemed to settle back in happily and all continued normally until this bizarre change in behavior.

Six months after she returned, she developed a false pregnancy (a normal part of the canine reproductive cycle).

However, the hormonal changes triggered complex emotional responses. Intellectually, Sarah understood that she was safe at home and probably would never be sent away again, but underneath she was petrified of the possibility of a repeat performance. Despite complex emotions and horrible circumstances, a case like this is often relatively easy to resolve. Sarah was willing — even anxious — to talk to me in order to have her fears and emotions understood by her person; she knew this was the key to her healing.

I suggested some Bach Flower Essences for her emotional support, which included aspen to treat the fear of being sent away; mustard for heavy sadness; olive for exhaustion, worry and the false pregnancy; star of Bethlehem to help overcome the prior traumatic whelping experience and walnut for transition.

I also suggested that Sarah and her person have a cathartic heart-to-heart talk and a good cry to alleviate both the hurt and the guilt.

Finally, I suggested Sarah's person accompany her outside when she needed to go so that Sarah had the time to do what she needed to. Her anxious impulse to hurry back inside, before she was finished, (which led understandably to "accidents" inside) dissipated.

The next day, I received an e-mail from Sarah's owner saying that they had had their talk and cry and that Sarah had begun to play with the other dogs again.

Several weeks later, I asked how Sarah was doing. "Oh, she's fine she said, "totally back to normal!"

A Relationship Blossoms

The developing relationship between one of my clients and her cat has been a joy to watch. For her, however, the road has been somewhat lumpy!

A woman I'll call Sally, called me initially because her cat, Dolly, was dying. We had several talks, which eased Dolly's transition.

Several months later, Sally went to the shelter and brought home a handsome orange longhaired cat we'll refer to as Oscar. Oscar was loving and affectionate, but there were two problematic issues. The first was that Sally missed Dolly so much that she couldn't stop wishing she would come back. Having another cat just wasn't the same. The second was that Oscar had been an outdoor cat and missed this part of *his* life as much as Sally missed Dolly. Oscar's frustration was voiced continuously and *loudly* at all hours of the day or night. Fortunately for everyone, no complaints were heard from any of the condo neighbors despite the fact that this story encompasses a nine-month period!

Sally lives in a city, so allowing Oscar the freedom to come and go was not an option. During one conversation, we discussed acclimating him to a harness and leash so they could go for walks together. Sally bought Oscar $37.00 worth of a lovely blue harness and matching flexi leash. For several weeks they practiced walking up and down the halls, then Sally felt they were ready to face the world. Within 30 seconds of being outside, Oscar twisted, turned, somersaulted and, like Houdini, was free. Sally regaled me with several hilarious (to me) stories of the Big Chase and their forays into the sewer system where she was able to retrieve him.

Four harnesses later, Oscar seemed to accept his restricted freedom. Sally writes: "The most fun he had was winding the leash around a large tree and a dozen low branches; then he lay down next to the tree to watch me run around to untangle the cord."

Sally tells a good story, but underneath was considerable frustration on both sides about the relationship. Sally continued to wish Oscar was Dolly, and Oscar continued to miss the control he used to have over his own life. Sometimes he screamed loudly in the middle of the night in an effort to get Sally to take him outside. There was a pretty low period when Sally made comments like, "Oscar's not a happy cat" and "We feel absolutely nothing for each other." and "I liked him better when he first came." I seriously wondered if perhaps they *would* both be better off with another arrangement. My counsel was that I thought they could work it out, but it wouldn't be smooth and the road began with a genuine commitment to each other on both sides.

The tide then began to turn, albeit slowly. I received a letter from Sally some weeks later ending with "Who knows—as the song says, 'For all we know, love may grow'."

Periodically, Sally calls me, mostly to sound off about Oscar's very loud mouth at inappropriate hours. Oscar told me during one conversation that his mission was to bring change to Sally's life. Each difference of opinion they have begins like a summit conference with the participants polarized. Fortunately, both are learning the fine art of compromise and often they have resolved the problem between the time the appointment is made with me and the appointment itself.

One issue Sally mentioned recently was that Oscar runs wildly through the house at 3 AM. She says she takes a feather pillow and bats him with it. He loves it! Now it's become a great game! I often tell people to watch their animals if they want to learn the best training techniques. Who has trained whom, here??

It's still not all smooth sailing, but I believe they are becoming an "item". These were Sally's words during her last call to me: "I've met more people in the neighborhood since I got this cat than in the previous 14 years and I look forward to our walks, now. It's relaxing." And the best: "I sort of love Oscar, now."

Sharing Space

Sometimes animal lovers call me because they want to share their space with animals, but the animal's behavior is irksome, or even antagonistic, which tends to make living together very difficult.

For instance, let me introduce Linda, who dearly loves her garden. When she described her garden to me it sounded quite elaborate, with stone paths and different sections for various flowers and herbs.

Gizmo, her neighbor's cat, shares her appreciation of the garden, but his way of expressing his appreciation has left Linda distressed. She goes to a lot of effort to make the garden beautiful and ordered, then looks out the window to see Gizmo digging furiously, throwing soil and rocks in many directions.

Now, Linda likes Gizmo a lot and says he's a "neat cat," but she sees his behavior as destructive. She's become so frustrated and angry at him that one time, she confessed, she threw a stone at him but, she said, after it hit him, he turned around and played with it! She was at her wit's end when she called me for advice.

Together we decided to take a different approach. First, we acknowledged Gizmo for being such a great companion and for sharing Linda's love of the garden. Next, we decided that Linda should set aside a special area of her garden especially for Gizmo. Actually, since he liked soft earth, she got sawdust from the barn for him to dig in.

This strategy appears to have worked out very well, since Gizmo now spends most of his time in the fields, hunting and being a cat. When Linda goes out to garden, Gizmo appears and they spend time together, each gardening in his or her own way, each in his or her own space.

Usually, when animals use what people consider "their own" space, the animals simply aren't aware that their actions are being perceived as destructive or negative. The cats who use your garden as a bathroom or the deer who eat your flowers are only doing what comes naturally. When a different point of view is explained to them they're generally very willing to modify their behavior.

Rhoda and I worked out a compromise with the deer who were eating her flowers. She really enjoys having the deer visit every day, but is distressed to find her flower buds eaten each morning. Since she didn't want to ask the deer to leave all together, Rhoda designated a portion of her garden for the deer and asked that they leave her part alone.

At first, the plan was simply to give the deer a certain part of her foliage to eat, but they pointed out that they could get this plant anywhere. Certain flowers that were a delicacy to them were what drew them to her yard.

If we had not solicited input from the deer before coming up with the final plan, the plan wouldn't have worked. Once Rhoda decided she could part with some of her flowers in return for some remaining untouched, the plan was acceptable to the deer and, the following year she planted more bulbs specifically for them!

In another case, I really can't remember if we offered the roaches in Judy and Bob's apartment anything special; even I was amazed that they just picked up and left after a simple request to do so! Maybe they were so cooperative because they tend to adapt so well to different living conditions and diets.

I've had less success with other types of insects, namely mosquitoes and ticks. Finding a compromise for them is difficult as they both need blood to carry on their species. Asking them not to bite constitutes a death sentence for them and it really isn't ethical to ask them to bite someone else. This poses a dilemma! Recently, someone suggested that I allow them to bite but ask them not to inject the factor that causes the itching.

In most cases the answer to living in harmony with nature—and the world in general—is to try to see the conflicting situation from the other being's point of view. Having done that, a solution to the discord will most certainly come to mind and usually turns out to be acceptable to both parties.

Chapter IV

Animals Speak! About Training

Animals deserve a lot of credit for learning anything from us at all! In general we are possibly the most unfocused of species! First, our minds race a mile-a-minute, second, we often don't pay attention to where our minds are going and third, we often think about more than one thing at a time! Have you ever tried to follow the conversation of a person who *talks* this way? Then you know what our animals have to wade through much of the time!

Several of the following stories have the same theme and the key to each situation lay in getting the *people* to pay attention.

Rocket, a Doberman Pinscher

Rocket was a ten-year-old black and tan Dobie who was just one "leg" away from the highest Schutzhund degree (a German-based obedience title) you can earn. Jill wanted to get the final leg, and thus the highest degree, so she could retire her dog who was aging.

Rocket had been doing all the exercises wonderfully, but all of a sudden he was having trouble on one part. "What was *wrong* with the dog?" she wanted to know.

The exercise in question involved the dog going into a tent and flushing out an intruder. It had to be handled with determination and enthusiasm, two qualities, which Rocket seemed to have forgotten. When I questioned Rocket on his change in behavior he told me that, for some reason, Jill had lost confidence in him. He said he listened to her for guidance and she wasn't sending the same confident signals he was used to. Evidently, Jill wanted the title so badly that she had begun to conjure up all kinds of senseless worries. She was focusing on

47

the areas where the dog could fail. In trying to take his cues from her, Rocket was, indeed, failing!

My suggestion to her was to watch some videos of dogs who were doing the exercise correctly. She said that was no problem because she had many such videos of Rocket himself performing flawlessly.   That was perfect! Jill was sent home with the directive to watch the videos and then run them through her head when she wanted him to do that work.

The plan worked so well that Jill's training instructor called me to set up a Talking with Animals Workshop so that they could incorporate my techniques into their regular training procedures.

I wish there were a fairy tale ending to the story, but in this case it didn't work out that way. Unfortunately, while Jill was able to concentrate when she wasn't under pressure to perform, she had a relapse under test conditions. Rocket performed well as long as Jill was relaxed, but was so close to her that he couldn't hold it together when Jill let down her half. As it turned out, Rocket was retired without getting the final leg and Jill learned a valuable lesson about the importance of her mindset and focus when working and showing her dogs.

Journey and Tom

Journey and Tom were incredible to watch working. Journey was a Thoroughbred horse and he and Tom were working at a high level of dressage. To the outside observer, their performance was breathtaking, but Tom felt the timing just wasn't quite right.

Tom's complaint was that Journey was changing to the next part of the routine just a little before Tom asked him to and this was throwing off the whole performance. Journey was surprised to hear this as he felt he was responding perfectly to Tom's requests. With just a tiny bit more questioning, it came out that Tom visualized the next move in his head just before asking Journey to execute it. This was the key, of course. Journey was so tuned into Tom that the moment the picture entered Tom's head, Journey performed. The "fix" was as easy as asking Tom to change his *own* timing. With this small adjustment in Tom's own thinking, their performance became perfectly synchronized.

Shirley and Axle

Shirley was an excellent dog trainer. She had trained many of her own Golden Retrievers to high-level obedience titles and also conducted classes to teach other people to train their dogs. The American Kennel Club (AKC) "go out" exercise was not a new one to her, one she had trained before, but for some reason, she was unable to get the concept across to her dog, Axle. When she came to my workshop, she was very frustrated since she had tried every approach she could think of.

After the workshop, Shirley took Axle out in the backyard. With him sitting next to her she visualized him doing a perfect go out. This simply means that, on cue, he was to leave her side, and walk away from her until she told him to sit. At that point he was to turn to face her and sit, waiting for the next cue. After visualizing it to herself, she gave the command. Axle not only flawlessly executed the exercise, but she told me she distinctly heard him say, "Why didn't you ever *say* that before?"

Betty and Paisley

One of the activities I participate in with my own dogs is AKC tracking. Paisley, a fawn Great Dane, was 11 months old when she obtained her Tracking Dog degree, the TD.

The track is a scent trail laid by a stranger to the dog. The tracklayer walks a pattern determined the previous day by the judges and leaves a glove at the end, which the dog must find. The track is from 450-500 yards long, 30 minutes to two hours old and must have three to five turns. The dog must follow the path of the tracklayer and indicate the glove to pass the test.

Paisley was a dynamite tracker, but she was sometimes a bit casual, preferring to extemporize at times, and she could easily be led astray by something interesting out in the field.

The test day was a beautiful May day but, for the purposes of a nervous dog handler, it was marred by a wind so strong I was literally blown off my feet more than once. Wind can do strange things to a scent and I was a nervous wreck thinking how easily my headstrong partner could be misled.

The first dog to run was a Chihuahua. The small dog had her own challenges, but I noticed that she was so close to the ground that the wind did not appear to be a factor in her tracking decisions. I realized that the key for Paisley was to convince her to be *sure* to keep her head down low.

With this in mind, I went back to the car to give her a "pep talk". Paisley assured me that she understood perfectly and admonished me to attend to my part. She said she could do it. We sat there a few moments longer while we visualized a perfect track and then went out to make it real.

Paisley was in her prime that day! With nose deep in the ground she set a pace so fast that it was all I could do to keep my own balance and stay behind her. Paisley earned her TD in style and gave quite a show to the people in the gallery who had come "to see the Dane track."

Alice and Myra

People who compete in AKC obedience events often bring crates to the obedience tent. This is where their dogs "hang out" until it is their turn in the ring. Fortunately, Myra, a Bernese Mountain Dog, already had completed the three legs necessary for her title and was going for an "insurance leg" since their performance this particular day was definitely unique.

One of the exercises the dog and handler are graded on is "heeling". The judge "calls the pattern" or tells the dog/handler team to start and stop, turn right, left or about turn and to halt. The dog is to walk at the handler's left side and the best teams look as though they are a well-rehearsed dance team as they perform in unison.

Alice and Myra had practiced countless hours and had performed this exercise flawlessly three times under three different judges but, this particular day, Myra took it into her head to "improve on the exercise," as she told me later. Instead of staying glued to Alice's side, she decided to do a tricky maneuver which allowed her to make a turn and meet up with Alice after Alice did the "about turn" on her own! Alice was very surprised at this turn of events and asked me to ask Myra what she was thinking.

As it turned out, from her crate under the tent, Myra had been talking to more experienced obedience dogs. They told her that the exercises never varied and that to jazz up the obedience experience a little, it was necessary for the dogs to become creative!

We all got a good laugh out of the experience and I learned why so many dogs who are competing at the highest levels often give non-qualifying performances. Myra didn't get to hang out in the tent much after that and Alice made it a point to continually teach new exercises so that Myra didn't make up her own program.

Myra is long gone now, but Alice and her new generation of dogs are working in Freestyle. Freestyle, or "dancing with your dog" is based in dressage and thrives on creativity of both dog and human. Myra's lesson lives on!

Chapter V

Animals Speak! About Grief

"There is a bridge connecting Heaven and Earth. It is called the Rainbow Bridge because of its many colors. Just this side of the Rainbow Bridge, there is a land of meadow, hills and valleys with lush green grass.

When a beloved pet dies, the pet goes to this place. There is always food and water, and warm spring weather. The old and frail animals are young again. Those who have been maimed are made whole. They play all day with each other.

But there is one thing missing. They are not with their special person who loved them on Earth. So, each day, they run and play until the day comes when one suddenly stops playing and looks up. The nose twitches! The ears are up! The eyes are staring! And this one suddenly runs from the group.

You have been seen, and when you and your special friend meet, you take him in your arms and embrace. Your face is kissed again and again and again and you look once more into the eyes of your trusting pet.

Then you cross the Rainbow Bridge together, never again to be separated."

The Rainbow Bridge, attributed to Paul Dahm

A bittersweet but extremely rewarding part of my work in talking with animals, I call "pre-grief" counseling, giving support prior to the pet's demise.

Many times we know when the end of our companion's life is approaching. We also know that being able to use euthanasia legally is a gift we can give our animals for the alleviation of suffering.

Confusion arises because none of us wants to lose an animal friend prematurely, nor do we want to prolong suffering needlessly. This dichotomy presents a fine line, which can sometimes lead to anxiety and guilt for the people involved. Often, I have been able to help people with their decisions by asking the animal in question what he or she thinks.

A woman, Julie, brought her wonderful canine companion to me. This dog had, in the course of the last two years, suffered two nearly fatal heart "attacks", but in each case had valiantly recovered to return to her owner. Now, she was in a severe decline and Julie needed to know if this was the time to let her go. In this case, the answer was "yes." What made this time different from previous episodes was that Julie had recently married. Earlier, the dog had felt she had to survive in order to take care of her person. Now, she was relieved because she loved and trusted the new husband and felt he could take over this responsibility. She was now ready to go.

Another time, a similar question turned out differently. In this case the dog had been extremely active all his life. He had been a frisbee champion and took an active role in guarding the property. Now, he was old and arthritic and his person wondered if the quality of life had deteriorated to the point where it was intolerable for her pet.

Interestingly, this dog had already modified his guard dog role and was very satisfied with it. Instead of dashing around the perimeter of the yard barking, he now stationed himself on a rug by the front door, at rest but still easily able to sound the alarm. The dog, Bear, did tell me he missed being able to play frisbee though. At my suggestion, the person began playing "hide and seek" with the frisbee inside the house. This way, Bear could "catch" the frisbee at his own pace.

This woman also took my "Talking with Animals" workshop. A year later, I got a wonderful letter from her telling me that, because of being able to talk to her dog, he'd been able to tell her when the time to go had truly arrived. His life concluded with peace and dignity in the arms of his best friend.

Most of the animals with whom we share our lives have shorter life spans than we do, so it is inevitable that we go through the trauma of losing them time after time in our lives. It's comforting to both the human and the animal and eliminates confusion at this time to talk together about the animal's desires.

Buster and Donna

Buster was a very old white Terrier/Poodle mix. Listening to Donna talk about him, I could tell that he'd been "hell on wheels" in his day, a very special companion, but when he came to me he was in dire straits. He was heavily sedated to stop his seizures — almost comatose.

Donna carried him in an infant carrier and she was up round the clock with him—giving him medication, trying to get a little nourishment into him and waiting for a spark of the old Buster which came in increasingly fewer intervals.

When Donna first brought Buster to me, I was at a loss about what to do, but it turned out that under all the medication, Buster's mind was still functioning. During the course of a session, Donna was able to contact him and connect with him in a way that had been missing since he had become so sick.

I started doing Therapeutic Touch on him while we talked and after several such sessions, Donna reported to me that she had been able to reduce his seizure medication. This was with the full approval and amazement of her veterinarian, who was at a loss as to how to further help Buster. With reduced medication came more frequent moments of clarity, which didn't improve Buster's overall condition, but did help Donna and Buster to have a few more cherished weeks leading up to the inevitable time of transition.

Buster had come into Donna's life at a difficult time—a time when she didn't even want a dog! Besides that, he had been, she told me, the wrong kind of dog for her, as well. Nevertheless, their bond had become deep and permanent. Our sessions allowed Donna to follow through on her commitment to Buster and to tie up loose ends before he crossed the Rainbow Bridge.

Savannah, Erica and Dave

Savannah walked into my office under her own power, but it was clear after only a few minutes that she was in very fragile condition. She was a German Shepherd mix who had been Erica's dog before she and Dave were married. She'd been a wonderful companion to them both for many years, but all three of them knew it was time for her to leave. The question was how to go about doing it.

The issues were complex. Neither Dave nor Erica wanted to be the one to make the decision, feeling that it somehow would impinge on the relationship they had with each other. Dave didn't want to be the one to euthanize "Erica's" dog and Erica was just plain having trouble dealing with the whole issue.

During the course of the consultation, Savannah was the moderator. It was heartwarming for me, as the interpreter, to see how she led first one and then the other to understand that she was ready to go. She gave them permission to help her and then started talking about the wonderful life she'd had with them. She talked particularly about the music. Upon questioning, I discovered that Dave was a songwriter and Savannah had been his "sounding board" during his work sessions.

The four of us worked out a plan whereby Savannah, Erica and Dave would deliberately spend time talking about all the good times, play some favorite music and then prepare for her passing.

A few weeks later, I got a thank you call. They wanted me to know our visit had allowed her transition to be "one of the most beautiful things we've done." It made me feel good to know that her memory would be a sweet one, with no regrets.

Grief Counseling

The grief counseling I do is for the animals. Sometimes they have lost a person; sometimes it's an animal friend. In either case, it can be profound and can impact their health and quality of life.

Libby and me

Waccabuc's Empire State, TD, or Liberty, also known as Libby, is the last of our original Waccabuc Great Danes line. She sits beside me at the age of 12 as I write this, but when I lost her daughter six years ago, I thought I was going to lose her too.

Piper was a lovely young Great Dane bitch and I was very close to her. I had whelped her and raised her. She was my good friend and my first dual titled dog: Waccabuc's Fife and Drum, CD, TD (Companion Dog and Tracking Dog). We were on our way to a conformation championship as well, but first she was ready to pass on her good qualities by becoming a mother. She was a week into her pregnancy when something happened.

We got up as usual, but when I went to call her from outside, she didn't come back. I went looking for her in the back yard and found her standing oddly, afraid to move. Together, we managed to get back to the house, but it was obvious something was very wrong. She stood stiffly with her back arched and her tail up in a very unnatural position. I checked for a variety of possibilities such as bloat (an emergency condition which affects Danes and other breeds), but couldn't pinpoint what was wrong.

Throughout the day, I consulted veterinarians and our chiropractor, but no one could shed any light on her plight. About three o'clock in the afternoon, Piper followed me onto the breezeway, collapsed, and died.

It was such a shock. I never expected that we were dealing with a fatal situation and I was devastated. I went through the motions of taking care of the other dogs for the next several days, but my mind was on Piper.

During this time, Libby stopped eating and then had diarrhea. Distractedly, I gave her some slippery elm, which usually helps with transient loose bowels. Then she started vomiting. This got my attention!

I sat down with her and we talked. She told me that she was also grieving the sudden loss of her daughter and that in her grief, she was unprepared to deal with how badly *I* was behaving. She didn't know how to cope with me being so out of control. We talked further about missing Piper and how some of the jobs she had done needed to be re-assigned. Piper had been the "official greeter" and Libby was willing to accept this job until someone else wanted it.

At the end of our conversation, Libby jumped up and went outside. Her physical symptoms ceased from that moment on.

Four months later, Piper sent Paisley to take over from her. It often happens that way...

Chapter VI

Animals Speak! About Things Out of this World

The Role of Animals
In Our Lives

One of the questions I am most often asked is about the place of animals in our lives. Indeed, animals who choose to live with people play a very special role. Most animals come to serve us in one capacity or another.

A young female cat named Pogo came to her person, Dave, at a difficult time in his life. Her role for the next 15 years was as a gentle "steering wheel" or guide—someone to talk to and lean on and someone with whom to share ideas, as strange as this might sound to some. On the other hand, another cat's purpose was to shake up the complacent life of her person and get her to move in a new direction.

When one of my dogs died prematurely and unexpectedly, she sent another to fill her "unexpired term". Evidently, I had had expectations that the first one couldn't fill, so I was given someone else better suited to the "job requirement!"

A Lhasa Apso named Emma was sent to help Laura along the spiritual path she had chosen, and came packaged in her small form to be able to travel with Laura on airplanes.

However, not every companion animal seems to have a higher purpose. Some may not have evolved to the point where they're ready for a dual role and they live their entire lives on the relatively uncomplicated physical plane. At times, this may seem to be the case, but if you talk to the animal at a different time in his/her life, you may get different information.

One dog I met recently has lived all of her 13 years in abeyance, waiting for her person to become aware. In the last few years, the woman has begun to realize that animals are individuals with feelings beyond those of "just a dog". Now, late in her life, the dog has started to fulfill her mission to guide her person to respect all species.

Sometimes when I ask an animal about his or her role or purpose, they know in amazing detail, but sometimes they seem confused as though the instructions given them were to go to a certain place and wait for more information, as though in the game of Treasure Hunt. As in the case above, the rest of the story will be revealed to them when the time is right.

Animals' purposes in our lives really can be anything, and sometimes it's useful to ask them, as the answer can be truly enlightening. Whatever the higher purpose is, however, we must remember to respect animals for themselves on the physical level, first for that is their primary purpose in being.

Out of This World

Most of the time, animals who come to me for help have reasonably "down-to-earth" concerns. We heal health-related situations (after appropriate veterinary care) with concrete suggestions—always beginning with a diet review.

Sometimes the appropriate technique to use is an energy approach such as Therapeutic Touch, Reiki, TTEAM or flower essences, or a combination of these. Sometimes just talking out a problem is what's needed.

Very occasionally, however, while these approaches are helpful, they aren't enough. It is for these times that I ask the animal, "Can you tell me about a past life which has bearing on the present situation?"

Four such stories come to mind. In each case, I was overwhelmed by the power these events had over the present day life of the animals and, in most cases, how dramatically their behaviors changed after we were able to bring the past into the realm of conscious thought.

The first story is the story of Lana, a very skittish calico cat who sat in Gayle's flower studio and ate dried flowers. Gayle was worried because, while she enjoyed the cat's company, she was afraid eating non-food material might intestinally block Lana.

The first time I talked with Lana, I didn't feel we had done more than scratch the surface of the problem. She told me she ate the flowers because they tasted good, which I interpreted as a superficial answer designed to placate humans. In any case, our meeting was not as productive as I would have liked and her behavior didn't change.

The next time we talked, I asked her about past lives. She transported me to a time when she had been a very creative (human) woman who loved to work with her hands. However, the social climate of the day did not look kindly on women with skills such as hers. She lived in fear of her life and resolved never to let herself be in such a situation again. In fact, when it was time to reincarnate, she came as a being with no hands so there would be no temptation to be creative.

Unfortunately, she now lived with a creative person, which proved to be a source of unending frustration to her. This frustration, in turn, led to her trying to be involved in the creative process by this odd and potentially dangerous manifestation of eating dried flowers. The fact that she had previously feared for her life in relation to her creative abilities came out in this life in her extreme skittishness.

A combination of telling me the story and Bach flowers for emotional support, were enough to turn her around. As soon as the next day, Gayle reported that Lana was now content to sit in the studio and watch, but didn't feel compelled to participate. "You know," she said, "she's much more friendly too!"

The next case is dramatically different. Taylor was physically one of the most handsome horses I've ever seen, but therein lay his problem.

He was a brilliant horse, but his temper was on such a short fuse that he was dangerous. One minute he was executing some intricate dressage move and the next he'd be rearing

63

uncontrollably, putting his rider at extreme risk. Some days he would viciously attack anyone who tried to enter his stall.

His story doesn't have the same happy ending that Lana's did, but understanding Taylor made a change in Judy's life.

Judy had sent me a picture of him, so when I first met him over the phone, I started by commenting on how handsome he was. His first response to me was an angry torrent. "Never asked to be this color." he said. "No one ever appreciates anything but my looks!" I answered him, "Can you tell me something good about you?" "I'm *smart!*" he shot back.

After several sessions and some recommendations designed to deal with Taylor's behavior in this life, I finally turned to asking about other lives. He was immediately forthcoming.

He told me about a lifetime as a retarded and deformed child who was taunted and abused. He grew up to be a violent man, a murderer in fact, and ended up in prison where more abuse followed.

When he reincarnated, he told me that he came back as the complete opposite—one who was physically beautiful and extremely intelligent. He thought this would be enough but he found that, once again, he was treated differently because of these attributes. He felt that he was still an outcast.

Taylor said he had come back as a horse to serve humans since he had abused them in his former life. However, he had never released the anger from before and the more separated he felt by people treating him differently, the more his anger escalated until he was just blindly reacting in rage.

Unfortunately, there wasn't time for some of the suggestions I made to be implemented before the daily danger of living with him became too much for his guardians. He went back into the horse trading system, once again for sale. I hope he wasn't the victim of abuse, or the cause of injury.

The one highlight of this sad tale, however, is that Judy resolved to do something positive as a result of all this. She told me that she was going to work with retarded people to help prevent others from harboring this type of anger.

The next story is about another cat. Gus was a big, fluffy Maine Coon-type cat. He was healthy, handsome and affectionate, but recently had taken to spraying in the house. Valerie, Gus' person, was open to talking about past lives, so I asked Gus to talk about this.

He told me that in a previous time, he had been Valerie's husband. He had come back as a cat to be with her once again, but was shocked and angered to find her in a gay relationship. He disapproved mightily of this arrangement and was voicing his strong opinion.

Two interesting things came from this conversation. Valerie said she was not at all surprised. In fact, she admitted that this revelation explained some other confusing behaviors between Gus and her partner. Further, once Gus voiced his disapproval of Valerie's lifestyle, he evidently was able to let it go. He didn't require any changes in the situation; he just wanted to make sure he was understood!

I never heard directly from Valerie again, but some time later she referred a friend to me. The friend reported that after his conversation with me, Gus never sprayed again!

The last story is that of Karma, a handsome Tibetan Terrier. He had been with his person, Sue, since puppyhood and had a wonderful, dog-oriented, understanding homelife. He competed in conformation dog shows and worked in obedience and agility. He had acres of land on which to exercise and in every way had outlets for all his mental and physical needs. Nevertheless, despite good training, adequate socialization and a good, natural diet, he was dog aggressive. Sue, also said that even from puppyhood, he "just seemed sad."

When I asked Karma about any past lives that might have had a bearing on this life, he was quick to respond with several different scenarios. He had been various types of "pack" animals from horses to humans, but the common thread was that he was always on the *outside* of the pack. In some cases, he had been purposely ostracized for one reason or another. In other cases, he held *himself* apart from the group.

As a dog, in this life, he said he was really trying to be a "team player", but it was very hard. He always had the subtle feeling that he didn't quite belong or that he wasn't *allowed* to belong.

Often understanding where the animal is coming from, and what parameters he is working within is the key to healing. In addition to talking about the problem, Karma and I chose some flower remedies to give him support. A more natural diet will help him to feel better both mentally and emotionally, as well. I know he and Sue now have the tools to begin to effect a change.

Talking about an animal's past lives may seem esoteric and, as I said, it isn't often that I work with it. Nevertheless, when other approaches fail, this has turned out to be a powerful technique.

Chapter VII

Animals Speak! About the Ten Commandments of Living with Animals

THOU SHALT ...

1. Talk to your pet every day.
2. Touch your pet every day.
3. Feed only nutritious food.
4. Teach your pet proper manners.
5. Provide a confined area for exercise and play.
6. Give your pet "private time" with you every day even if s/he has animal companions.
7. Be observant for health changes in your pet.
8. At least once a week take your pet away from the house to see the world,
9. Give your pet a job to do.
10. Treat your pet with the respect due all living creatures.

1. Talk to your pet every day.

Talking *to* our animals is nearly as important as talking *with* them. Taking the time to talk to your pets means focusing on each one as an individual. This makes them feel special and needed.

2. Touch your pet every day.

The second commandment, touching your pets, can be done simultaneously with the first. This is not a perfunctory pat on the head, however, or absent-minded stroking while you watch TV. Nor is it petting two dogs at one time while you scratch a third with your feet! Again, a few seconds of undivided attention is required! The length of time spent is not important, though a real massage is a wonderful way to enrich your relationship with your pets (see *Dr. Michael Fox's Massage Program for Cats and Dogs*). Remember to look at least weekly for any lumps, bumps, cuts, scratches or other changes to keep you aware of your pets' physical health. For those familiar with energy work, your pets appreciate this, too. It is a very beneficial part of your daily touch sessions.

3. Feed only nutritious food.

Feeding only nutritious foods is a topic unto itself and is the subject of many books. We have been led to believe that animals must eat commercial foods from a bag rather than the raw ingredients, which sustained them for thousands of years. This concept is entirely erroneous. (Check the "References" section for information and see the special chapter on feeding.)

4. Teach your pet proper manners.

Animals are different from humans, there's no denying it, but species most frequently seen as pets in our society have chosen each other precisely because they live so well together. People and animals get along much more happily when each respects the needs of the other. Animals feel comfortable knowing boundaries and it is your duty to teach them in a humane way. Don't let "but it isn't natural," be an excuse for unsuitable behavior that could easily be modified. Be sure to take time to teach proper house manners to your pets.

5. Provide a confined area for exercise and play.

A major killer of dogs and cats is the automobile. The average lifespan of an outdoor cat is six months, while I have known of indoor cats who have lived as many as 23 years. These statistics speak for themselves! We no longer live in environments where animals can safely be left to their own devices. Responsible pet guardianship requires that this subject be addressed for all pets.

I am often amazed at the people who say to me: "No, I don't have a fenced yard, but we live on five acres." Not good enough! Have you ever seen how quickly an animal can negotiate five acres? Don't leave your animals to the mercy of the roads, to being shot, being poisoned by irate neighbors, mauled by a larger dog or any of a hundred possible scenarios which happen every day.

6. Give your pet "private time" with you every day even if she has animal companions.

Commandment #6 is easiest to do if you only have one pet. It tends to happen almost automatically. However, it is just as important to have a one-on-one relationship with each animal in a multiple pet household on a daily basis, even when animals have "each other". Fortunately, we can take advantage of the fact that animals have a different sense of time than we do. They tend to live more in the present, so 15 minutes of quality time spent with one animal can be perceived as equal to all day with another, as long as it is "private time". Suppose you take one on a shopping trip and are gone all day. When you come home, you might spend 15 minutes throwing a ball for another and five minutes asking a third about his day and telling him about yours. You have just satisfied commandments #1, and possibly #2 as well!

7. Be observant for health changes in your pet.

#7 is on going of course, but can be incorporated into the time you spend touching your pet and most especially during the weekly grooming.

8. At least once a week, take your pet away from the house to see the world.

Especially since I recommend that your pets be confined for exercise and play when they are home, it is particularly important that they "get away" occasionally. Prepare your pets for this by teaching them to enjoy riding in the car. I pity the poor animals who never get out except to go to the veterinarian! If your pet can go with you when you do errands, their world can be greatly expanded. I have four Great Danes and some combinations of two go with me regularly. Do be sensible about the weather and don't leave a pet in the car when it is too hot or too cold.

A second suggestion is to teach your pet to walk on a leash. Most dogs are lead trained, but few cats are. Some cats won't tolerate it, and I don't suggest you start with your 14-year-old recluse, but most young kittens can learn to tolerate it well, and it opens many avenues otherwise closed. Nothing is too bizarre—I once knew someone who took her pet boa constrictor for walks on a leash! And the stories that snake could tell!

9. Give your pet a job to do.

Every individual needs a job to do to feel needed and worthy. Pets are no exception. Many animals naturally fall into their jobs, like guarding the house or watching the children. Others need to be guided. Be creative and find what your pet does best. One of our "official greeters" died and his responsibility was given to another. A year later, we got a new puppy. It was with great relief that everyone discovered that greeting came naturally to him. He received the "official" title and takes his position very seriously.

10. Treat your pet with the respect due all living creatures.

This commandment is the most important of all. The key to our relationship with our pets is to remember that we are not better than they, just different. If we are fair and respectful, we will gain from our associations with our pets. This holds true, of course, in our associations with all forms of life.

Chapter VIII

What is Telepathy?

Talking With Animals

Now that you've read all the stories about what is possible when you add the telepathic dimension to your life with animals, you're probably wondering how you can learn to do it yourself. As I said before, I firmly believe that all species, including humans, have this ability. Therefore, there is no reason why you can't do it. There are some techniques to learn and, the key to all skills, is practice.

What is telepathy?

First, it is a language. Just like English, Spanish, French, geometry, music or American Sign Language. It is a form of communication and, in this case, happens to be the *fundamental* language of all life.

Like any language, it can be learned, although, technically, this is a misnomer. It's more accurate to say it can be *re-learned*, since all life is born knowing how to use it innately. Human children are born with the ability to use it but unfortunately we begin to lose it when we start to concentrate on the spoken and written word.

Two events usually kill the skill altogether. The first is the adult parent who disbelieves the child who has conversations with her dog or other pets. It's very powerful when an adult tells us that something isn't possible. The more we hear that something is impossible, the more we begin to believe it ourselves until, finally, we think we are making up the conversations or information we get from Mother Nature's creatures. The second is when we go to school. There is so

75

much emphasis on the spoken and written word to the exclusion of all else that we bury our telepathic abilities, sometimes never to be seen again.

I always take a poll in my workshops to see what percentage of people have been brainwashed by this emphasis on verbal skills and I'm happy to report that excessively verbal people like myself are in the minority. When someone says the word "dog" to me, I literally see the word "D-O-G". This is the same with most nouns. I literally see the *word* in my head. Fortunately, it turns out, most people haven't been taught quite this thoroughly and instead, they see the *picture* of the animal. The good news is that if you are one of the majority who sees the picture, re-learning telepathy should be especially easy for you. If you, like me, are a "dedicated verbal" person, it's still not that hard. You will have to go through an extra step in the beginning, but once you've taught yourself to skip the word itself, you'll be using this skill like a pro.

The definition of telepathy is the sending and receiving of pictures, thoughts and feelings using mental energy. How the information comes to you will depend on your own strengths and the strength of the individuals you're talking to. For example, you take in information using *all* your senses: visual, auditory, tactile, olfactory, taste, and kinesthetic (feeling), but you will find some senses easier to perceive than others.

In general, humans are visual beings. Some are very highly refined in this area. If this is your area of strength, you will find telepathy to be very easy and rewarding. You may "see" information in your mind either as a still or moving picture. Sometimes you'll see specific details as well. People with highly developed visual senses are very impressive when they describe what the animals are saying. However, while each of us is capable of perceiving from all the senses, different people find they are stronger in different senses. *However you receive the information, realize that it is valid. This is very important. There is no "wrong" way to perceive information.* You just have to learn your strengths and weaknesses. Once you understand this, you work to maintain your strengths and strengthen your weaknesses.

My kinesthetic sense is my strongest. Once I learned to accept that my instinctive way to understand another being was through feeling their happiness, sadness, pain, frustration, or any other emotion, I could relax and enhance the telepathic experience by concentrating on the other senses.

Dogs particularly are, in general, olfactory beings. Since for humans the sense of smell is a very weak sense, this is one it pays to develop. You won't necessarily increase your own ability to smell, but you *will increase* your appreciation of what is possible to know through smell. You'll smell in your mind, not with your nose!

The language of telepathy is instantaneous. As soon as a question is formed in your mind, you have the ability to get the answer. Sometimes this means you will miss the answer because you weren't ready to hear it. Sometimes it will seem as though there is a delay and you may think you missed the answer or the animal didn't understand the question. Any of this may be so, but it may also be true that the animal has to ponder the question before knowing, and sending the answer. If I ask you what your favorite color is, do you know right away? Some people do. With others, preferences change. You may have to consider it a moment. And, your favorite color is a pretty easy, straightforward question. If I asked you what you consider your mission in life, a question people *often* ask their animals, how long might it take you to answer?

Telepathy is a natural language. It is one animals use to communicate among themselves. Watch your animals to see evidence of this. Animals also listen to our thoughts when it is advantageous to them to do so. When I worked in the veterinary hospitals, it was interesting to keep track of the cats who disappeared the day of their appointment. They only reappeared when it was too late to reschedule for that day based on the information they got from the minds of their humans. Veterinarians and groomers know that most animals are much easier to work with when their anxious owners aren't present. The animals pick up worry from their people, wonder what is wrong, and act accordingly.

I had to cure myself of the habit of planning my time in my head. In the beginning, it took several times before I understood just how tuned in my dogs were to me. I remember saying to myself, "I'll finish this chapter and then go out with the dogs." Within *seconds* I had several dogs in "my face" wanting me to go out. I finally learned that if I wanted to finish the chapter, I had to keep my mind quiet!

Because this is a universal communication method, it is useful in circumstances other than talking to animals. This is outside of the scope of this book, but it is useful to know that it has been used successfully with pre-verbal infants, including those not yet born, stroke victims who have lost their ability to talk, people who have lost their speech through accidents such as head injuries, and autistic children.

The next chapter will focus on exercises you can do to learn how to *send* and *receive* information, the basis of telepathic communication.

Animals Speak!

Chapter IX

Exercises in Telepathy

Communication consists of two parts, sending information and receiving information. When you send information, you think about the topic and use all your senses to transfer what you want the other party to know. In sending, *you* make up images. In receiving, someone else makes up the information and you open your mind to "hear" it. Theoretically, it's as simple as that!

Exercises in Sending

Concentration and focus are often easier when your eyes are closed, so close your eyes and spend several minutes doing the following sending exercises.

1. Visualize your living room.

Put your mind on soft focus and get a general impression of your room. Note smells, sounds, colors and the feel of the atmosphere. Then, using your mind's eye as a zoom lens, focus on various parts of the room, pieces of furniture, knick-knacks. Even look out a window. Try to experience all the details you can.

2. Pretend you are calling your animal to come to you.

See your animal friend in her normal environment. See yourself calling her. See the expression on your animal's face as she comes flying to you.

81

3. Imagine the following, using all your senses to make each image as real as possible.

a roaring fireplace
plunge your hand into an ice bucket
walk through a flower garden
walk through the perfume department of a store
lie on the beach and close your eyes, listen to the sounds
look through a kaleidoscope
imagine a rainbow
take a cold shower
drive to the grocery store in your mind
count all the windows in your house

The only thing left after becoming adept at creating scenarios in your mind is the intangible "projection" of these images. Basically, the intent for another to receive them is all that's needed. You don't have to do anything tricky or hard.

Exercises in Receiving

Receiving requires that you have an empty mind and that you be aware of all sensations. In my workshops, we spend considerable time determining each person's strengths and weaknesses. Humans as a species tend to be visually oriented, so this is a place to begin. When you do the following exercises, pay attention to what sensations were easiest to perceive and which were the hardest. Then practice learning the ones which were difficult until they come easily.

1. Read the following story feeling all the sensations, hearing the sounds, seeing the images, tasting and smelling whatever is there to be experienced.

The Dog Show

It is a beautiful day. The sun is out, the sky is a lovely deep blue and there is a subtle breeze blowing to keep the air invigorating. You can feel the warmth of the sun on your skin, but your overall perception is of how perfectly comfortable you are. It's a perfect day for a dog show, pleasantly warm, yet cool and invigorating too.

You are early, so you park your car in the shade and arrange the windows so your dog will be able to rest comfortably while he waits for you. Then you collect your belongings to take to ringside. You take a chair, a green lawn chair, and a yellow umbrella, which attaches by a clamp to the back of the chair. You also take your red and white cooler, which is filled with ice & water.

The rings are over a hill from the wooded, shady parking area. As you reach the top of the hill, you can see the gigantic blue and white striped tent, which is set up in a field. Beneath the tent, the rings are side by side. The rings are made of wooden yellow baby gates connected by blue triangular stanchions.

You set up your chair by a ring and sit down to watch a few breeds before it's time to go get your dog. It is a few minutes to 9:00 and judges are walking around examining their rings. The judge in front of you, a man in a plaid sportcoat, picks dandelions that have popped up on the freshly mowed grass.

Everything is peaceful. Now, there is an announcement over the p.a. system: "Good morning ladies and gentlemen. Please pause for the national anthem." The Star Spangled Banner blares from a loud speaker. An occasional dog barks. Then the show begins.

You resume your seat. The first class enters the ring. Suddenly, the terrified yelping of a Basset Hound a few feet to your left shatters the mood. The owner is in a panic and begins to shriek. The dog is making the most awful noises, too. You look over and immediately notice a bee in the last moments of his life lying on the ground near a dandelion at the dog's feet. You immediately realize that the dog has been stung.

You rush over, take a deep breath and calm the 12-year-old blonde girl holding the dog. You tell her you will try to help. You turn your attention to the dog and ask it to hold still so you can help. Then you flip the right front paw back so you can see the stinger at the edge of the pad. Easily, you pick the stinger out You pull your cooler to you and plunge the dog's foot into the ice water. Instantly the heat and stinging sensation leave the foot.

The crisis is over, judging resumes; the atmosphere is, once again, business as usual.

Now that you have read the story, go back again and see what sensations came easily to you and what you had to stretch to experience. *This exercise is the crux of the whole technique!* The more you can experience easily, the more open you will be to receive pictures, thoughts and feelings that are sent to you. You might even want to tape record this, or paragraphs from a book and listen to them each day until you can experience all your senses mentally. In my workshops I use the book *Clan of the Cave Bear* by Jean Auel for this, but you can use anything that has good imagery.

In the next section, I will describe the steps to communication.

Chapter X

The Steps

For ease of discussion, I have broken down the technique of telepathic communication into arbitrary parts or 6 steps. There are not actually "steps" in communicating; it all really flows together, but here they are anyway. I will discuss each separately.

1. Be present
2. Create a conducive environment
3. Establish contact
4. Send the message
5. Receive an answer
6. Acknowledge the answer

1. Be present

It is important, no matter whom you are talking to, that you leave extraneous chatter behind you. Pay attention! Become still and focused and in the present. In Therapeutic Touch (an energy healing technique developed by Delores Krieger, RN, PhD) this is called Centering. Since I have training in TT, I tend to use the Centering technique automatically to focus before talking to animals as well. You can use anything that works for you.

Here is a suggestion:

Centering

To prepare yourself for your conversation, clear your mind of extraneous thoughts and focus on the present. Sit down, close your eyes and wait for your mind to clear. If you find chatter coming back in, set it aside. Clear your mind and your body of tension, feelings, personal concerns, etc.

Take a few deep breaths, concentrating on breathing in calmness and allowing tension, fatigue, worry, etc. to leave with each exhaled breath.

Continue breathing in calmness and breathing out everything else until this is all you are doing and nothing intrudes to distract you.

Then you are ready to talk to animals.

2. Create a conducive environment

Sit quietly with the animal you are going to talk to. The TV should be off, the kids away from the house and the telephone answering machine taking your calls. You don't have to have perfect silence, but you do need a time when you are both being together in the moment.

Don't try to talk to an animal when she is obviously doing something else, either. When the postal carrier comes to the door and all the dogs are barking, this is *not* a good time to send mental "be quiet" messages. No one is listening!

Also, if you have multiple animals, it's best to start with one at a time.

Go into a room with just one animal.

3. Establish contact

It is important to do something to make the animal aware that you are going to do something different from your normal behavior. You can call her name or touch her or just say, "Hi". It's not necessary to be elaborate.

Sometimes the animal will look at you, sometimes not. In fact, I feel that *not h*aving eye contact is better. Staring into an animal's eyes is a different kind of body language than looking into a person's eyes. The meaning can be misinterpreted and it can be plain distracting. Sometimes, dogs especially, *will* stare at you or stare and bark or whine. When this happens, the person's response is often to try to "figure out" what the dog is saying. You are now concentrating on what *you* are thinking and missing the message entirely. Under these circumstances, it's actually better to look away, break eye contact and open your mind, to let the message come to you.

Sometimes animals will lie down and appear to be asleep. Cats particularly do this. If they really *are* asleep, you will not be able to talk to them, but if you look closely, you'll likely see an ear twitch or a partly open eye. The animal is quite receptive under these circumstances.

4. Send the message

As we did in the exercise on "sending" in the last chapter, visualize the message you want to send. Add as much detail and use as many of your senses as possible without spending an overly long time on creating the message. Then, have the "intent" to send the message.

Be clear in what you're sending. For example, if you're trying to ask your dog to "come" to you, send the image of her coming toward you. If she normally doesn't come on the first call when you call her in English, a common mistake is to immediately think to yourself, "Oh she probably won't come." What you've done is to send *two* messages: come and don't come. She now has the option to respond to either suggestion.

Remember, telepathy is not mind control. Your animal has free will and you cannot *make* her come just because you have sent the message telepathically. However, sending the message in the animal's "native language" makes the communication clear. It's as if I asked you, a native American speaking person, to "come over here" in French, a foreign language to you. You might even think you have the gist of the request, but when it's made in English, there's no doubt in your mind.

Sometimes verbalizing helps clarify your message, too. Usually, I find that when people say something out loud, for the moment that they're talking, there is no room for anything else in their mind. This will help train you to be simple and clear in your message.

Verbalizing led me to an embarrassing experience once, though, so I caution you to be careful what you say out loud.

In this instance, the dog, a German Shepherd mix was being asked what she thought of the person's new husband. I immediately got the image of a nice looking, tall, slender, dark-haired man. I described the person to the woman and she said, "No, that's not him, but I know who it is. He's a friend." So, I turned to the dog and said out loud, "Not that man, but the one who sleeps over." There was suddenly an embarrassed silence as the lady and I realized that the dog had told me that the first man had also "slept over." Now I try to be discreet in my verbalizations!

5. Receive an answer

To receive an answer, your mind must be empty. If you're still "sending" or you're wondering if the animal "got it" or if your mind is racing on to other things, you'll miss it.

The single biggest error in receiving an answer is *trying too hard.* It's difficult to explain, but you must "let it come to you". You can't "make it happen". Don't try to "push the river".

If you truly don't get anything at all, you can ask again. Also, consider the possibility that the answer is "no," "nothing," or "I don't know".

In my workshops, the most common comment people make is, "I don't know if I just made up the answer myself." Unfortunately, no, you can't know for sure. In the beginning, you must go on faith. Just *assume* that you got the answer from the animal. After a while, there is a certain feeling that goes along with this type of communication that you will recognize. This reinforces that you are actually talking to the animals.

6. Acknowledging the answer

Sometimes this is a formal "thank you," other times, just recognition that the animal has taken the time to talk with you. It's a matter of common courtesy. Also, it may solidify the idea that *you* are trying to talk to her. Our pet animals listen to *us* all the time, but they're in the habit of ignoring the possibility of two-way communication. With some animals, it may take a few tries to make her believe you really are trying to talk.

Above all, I leave you with two words:"confidence" and "patience". It takes both to be able to master this technique.

In the next chapter, I'll give some tips that might turn out to be useful.

Betty Lewis, RVT, Dr. A.N.

Chapter XI

Tying up Loose Ends

So that you don't have to reinvent the wheel, here are a few suggestions that will help you evaluate your conversations with animals.

Use positive statements

Neither the animals we're talking to, nor other humans, easily assimilate the negative. Nevertheless, our English language abounds with negatives. In the early days of giving my workshops, I used to try to discuss this part totally in positive terms, but I found that it's not feasible. There are so many negatives in our language that I found I couldn't eliminate them and still make any sense!

However, in the shortened version we use talking to animals, it's a good thing to strive for. For example, if you don't allow your dog to get on the furniture, what do you say when you find her on the couch? If you say, "Don't get on the couch," what are you really focusing on in your mind? You're visualizing, "Get on the couch!" I always laugh when I hear dog trainers telling people to say "No bark" or "No sniff" since that just reinforces what the dog is already doing. Yeah, the dogs get it eventually, probably because it's combined with the aversive collar "correction". For our purposes, however, it's more humane and more effective to say "Get on the floor," "Be quiet," and to give some other cue that will direct the nose from sniffing to another behavior.

Avoid the tendency to interpret

Describing what you see or feel or otherwise get from the animal is the most accurate way to discuss the conversation. We all come from our own experiences and we can only understand information when it's colored by our own lives. Therefore, it's probably impossible to totally avoid interpretation, but the less you inject *yourself* into the response the more accurate you will be.

Here is an example of what I mean:

At one of my workshops, Drummer, the brindle guy who had the fall I discussed in the chapter on healing, was talking to a student. We asked him what special activity he was involved in. The student replied that she felt he worked with children. If I had simply told her, "No, that's not it," she would have felt that she hadn't received the right information. In fact, she had. She had simply interpreted it wrong. I asked her to describe what she was seeing and she said she saw faces at his eye level. From there, she assumed we were talking about children. What he really did was to act in the capacity as a Therapy Dog at nursing homes. The people were either bedridden or in wheelchairs. Since he was a Great Dane, that put him at their eye level.

Give the animal a chance to think out a response

Sometimes the information will come to you so quickly it goes right through your head and you may miss it if you're not paying attention. And, sometimes, the animal needs to think out a response. You'll have to feel your way on this one and learn to recognize when you're not getting an answer and when to be patient.

How do I shut it off?

Especially in the realm of physical things, it's too easy to take on the feeling and make it your own. Since the animals' headaches, stomach aches and other aches and pains are usually felt in your *own* body, if you don't have a mechanism for eliminating them, you can make yourself uncomfortable.

It's simple to turn it off, but you have to remember to consciously *do* it! Simply say to yourself, "If this headache isn't mine, I'd like it to leave." It will be gone instantly. If you dwell on it, however, it can become your own. In that case, no amount of aspirin or whatever you might use for headaches will relieve it. If this happens a time or two, hopefully it will trigger you to remember to ask it to leave before it becomes annoying.

What is the best way to practice?

While most people want to learn to communicate with animals in order to talk with the animals they live with, I've found that it appears to be the most difficult to talk to your own animals at first. I think this is because we already know too much about them. It is easy to assume and project what you think they are trying to say.

Therefore, if at all possible, you might start with the animals who live with friends or with wild animals. All the while, keep trying with your own animals and it will eventually all come together.

How do I ask about health issues?

I generally try to do this in a systematic manner. This can be done in several ways. You can start at the head and work back, or you can start with a system such as the skeletal system and follow through until you're finished. Then start on another system. I concentrate on the animal, but am aware of the feeling showing up in my own body.

Some animals are extremely intuitive about their bodies. Sweet Dreams, the horse I talked about earlier, is such an animal. He was able to send me a detailed picture of his tendon injury that was later confirmed. Other animals, just like many people, have no real understanding of their bodies. They can tell you "where it hurts", but that's about all. Remember individual variability when you're asking about health.

If you don't know about the internal workings of the body, I would suggest that you don't try to evaluate how it's working. Let's consider that to be advanced work. You can get plenty of information from just asking the animal how it feels. You can pick up aches and pains and stiffness and nausea as well as many other things without getting too complex. These clues will be extremely valuable to a health care practitioner in deciding on a course of treatment.

Remember the animal's perspective

With the exception of horses, most companion animals are smaller than we are. Remember that a boulder may look like a mountain to a cat or a Chihuahua. If you forget this, you'll find that you doubt the information you get, which will only serve to undermine your faith in your ability.

Talking to animals telepathically is a two-way street. You only need to hold a thought in your mind with the intention that it go to the intended recipient, and then clear your mind for the answer. That's all there is to it!

Now, you have all the tools you need to go out and listen when the Animals Speak!

The following sections are not about talking with animals telepathically, but they are a part of good husbandry for holistic animal caretakers. In fact, the topics of species appropriate nutrition for animals and suitable vaccination protocols are fundamental to the health of our animal companions. I have put these chapters in the Appendix portion since they are technically outside the scope of this book, but, like the Resource section, I feel it is critical to provide this information to my readers.

Betty Lewis, RVT, Dr. A.N.

Appendix I

Vaccinations

This is an extremely controversial topic. My purpose, however, is not to give you direction, but to raise questions which cause you to examine the conventional protocols.

Commonly, puppies and kittens are given vaccines every two weeks starting at about 6 weeks. The vaccines contain up to 7 viruses in one syringe. When vaccines were a new modality, there was only one, for distemper, and that was given at 8 and 12 weeks. True to the American ethic "more is better", we are now bombarding immature immune systems and starting earlier. Even the conventional medical establishment is beginning to question this procedure.

In the March 1996 issue of the Animal Health Newsletter from Cornell University, there was a column entitled 'Rethinking Vaccination'. In it, Drs. Carmichael and Scott, experts in the field, discuss a paper presented in the Journal of the American Veterinary Medical Association entitled "Are we vaccinating too much?" The article explores the use and over-use of vaccines.

They suggest that some vaccines offered short-lived immunity (bordatella, leptospirosis, parainfluenza) and therefore annual boosters might be necessary. However, they felt that the need for annual boosters for parvovirus and distemper has not been established. The article also talked about why vaccines fail and the safety of vaccines, not only from the perspective of vaccine reactions, but also vaccine-induced tumors.

In a paper presented to the American Holistic Veterinary Medical Association (AHVMA) in 1993, Richard Pitcairn, DVM, PhD (immunology) wrote an article outlining his hypothesis that many of the chronic diseases we see today appear to be chronic expressions of acute diseases of yesterday. Years ago, animals either died of an acute disease or recovered. Today, he feels that vaccines give chronic versions of the acute diseases.

His charts on several canine and feline diseases are most thought provoking. For example, a symptom of acute canine distemper is watery discharge of eyes and conjunctivitis. The chronic expression is seen in many animals today in the form of chronic conjunctivitis, eye discharge and entropion.

Before blindly subjecting your new family member to a barrage of viruses, preservatives and other dangerous ingredients, consider asking your veterinarian to space out the vaccinations and eliminate ones which are ineffective or where there is little risk of exposure. Do make copies of articles you read and take them to your veterinarian. Sharing your knowledge will make working with your vet an easier task.

For further reading, look in a bookstore or library for *DPT: A Shot in the Dark* by Coulter, Harris, Fisher and Loe, *The Case Against Immunizations* by Richard Moskowitz, *The Vaccination Connection* by Sue Marston, *Immunization, and the Reality Behind the Myth* by Walene James.

The year 2000 brought with it come some exciting new healthy attitudes for our animal friends. By being informed at the start of a new life, you can help to insure that they will be with you to the maximum their genetics will allow. Feed optimally, make health choices that tilt the scale in the direction of well being and longevity, and train with respect. With all these areas covered, you cannot help but have a wonderful experience with your animal friends.

*Note: As of 1998, there have been some changes in the recommendations by certain veterinary schools. These changes will help our animals. They are a good first step.

This is the message sent out by Colorado State University discussing their new policy:

"New Vaccination protocol being recommended by Colorado State University A recent survey by one of the largest vaccine manufacturers (Pfizer) of small animal vaccination practices found 1,700 different vaccination recommendations for dogs and cats from veterinarians across the US. In January 1998 the CSU Veterinary Teaching Hospital will be offering its clients one additional vaccination program. We are making this change after years of concern about the lack of scientific evidence to support the current practice of annual vaccination and the increasing documentation that over vaccinating has been associated with harmful side effects. Of particular note in this regard has been the association of autoimmune hemolytic anemia with vaccination in dogs and vaccine-associated sarcomas in cats.....both of which are often fatal. Boosters, the annual re-vaccination recommendation on the vaccine label is just that....a RECOMMENDATION, and is not a legal requirement, except for rabies. The only commonly used vaccine that requires duration of immunity studies be carried out before licensure in the U.S. is rabies. Even with rabies vaccines, the label may be misleading in that a 3-year duration of immunity product may also be labeled and sold as a one year duration of immunity product.

Based on the concern that annual vaccination of small animals for many infectious agents is probably no longer scientifically justified, and our desire to avoid vaccine-associated adverse events, in January of 1998 we will be recommending a new immunization protocol to our small animal clients.

This program recommends the standard 3 -shot series for puppies (parvovirus, adenovirus 2, parainfluenza, distemper), and kittens (panleukopenia, rhinotracheitis, calicivirus) to include rabies after 12 weeks of age in cats and 16 weeks of age in dogs. Following the initial puppy and kitten immunization series, cats and dogs will be boostered one year later and then every 3 years thereafter for all the above diseases. Similar programs to this one have been recently adopted by the University of Wisconsin, Texas A & and the American Association of Feline Practitioners.

Other available small animal vaccines may need more frequent administration (Bordatella, feline leukemia, Lyme, etc.)

and may be recommended for client animals on an "at risk" basis. Recent studies clearly indicate that not all vaccines perform equally and some vaccine products may not be suitable for such a program."

Appendix II

Dog Nutrition: Two Articles

Nutrition for Companion Carnivores
(Note; this discussion specifically talks about dogs, but is applicable to cats & ferrets as well.)

Introduction

Until recently zoologists classified dogs and wolves as separate species; now scientists have proclaimed that there is no differences between the two species. This change was formalized in the 1993 publication: Mammal Species of the World, A Taxonomic and Geographic Reference, edited by D.E.Wilson and D.A.M. Reeder, published by the Smithsonian Institution in association with the American Society of Mammalogists.[1] This reference book is the final authority of the scientific community on mammal classification.

Why is this important in a discussion of nutrition for our pet dogs? In many ways, dogs are wolves with a thin veneer of civilization over them. We can learn a lot about our companion dogs from studying the wolves, but this discussion shall be confined to how best to feed our family companions using the wolf as a model.

What's wrong with commercial foods?

The number one item which makes commercial foods inappropriate for pets is that these foods are cooked. No one has ever reported seeing wild animals routinely barbecuing their meals! Raising the temperature of food above 118° destroys all the enzymes and many of the nutrients.

In addition, I am given to understand that in order for the extruder (machine that makes the kibble into little pieces) to work, the food must be at least 40% grain. Since there has never been a report indicating that dogs and cats require carbohydrates, let alone grains, the reliance on this inappropriate food source is out of proportion and detrimental to their health.* Many dogs who have had grains entirely eliminated from their diets have responded by having "allergies" and other conditions clear up.[2]

The best guide to feeding dogs is to think about what they would eat in the wild, and then to try to reproduce that as closely as possible with the ingredients we have available. Wolves eat whole animals, from mice to caribou, and supplement their diets with other things that they find, like over-ripe fruit that has fallen to the ground, grasses, seeds, nuts and vegetable matter. Very little grain would be found in the diet of a wild carnivore, and they would avoid the moldy, toxin-ridden grains that comprise the majority of commercial pet foods. Despite the fact that there is no evidence showing that dogs & cats require carbohydrates in their diets, that is what makes up most commercial foods.

From Sandra Brigola, editor and publisher of Canine Health Naturally Newsletter, comes the following information regarding commercial pet foods: "The stored grains are sprayed with ethoxyquin, and moldy grains that have mycotoxins, aflotoxin or fusarium molds are hard to destroy. The allowable level in pet foods is 1.0 ppm (parts per million). The way that pet food manufacturers get around this is by mixing grains with higher levels of mycotoxins with grains of lesser levels; hopefully to reduce the higher levels. In its 1992 report, the Mycotoxin Committee of the American Association of Veterinary Lab Diagnostics said: "Virtually all animal foods contain at least some viable mold."[3]

In addition to substandard and heavily preserved grains, there is more bad news. The "meat" ingredient is not a whole cow or even a steak. This is what Marina Zacharias printed in her Natural Rearing Newsletter:

"The National Animal Control Association has estimated that animal shelters kill over 13 million household pets a year. Of this total, 30% are buried, 30% are cremated and the remaining 40%, about 5 million pets, are shipped to rendering factories to be recycled and used in pet food." [4] This information has been confirmed in great detail by Ann Martin in her book, Food Pets Die For. [5]

In his book, Give Your Dog a Bone, Ian Billinghurst, BV. Sc (Hons), B.Sc. Agr., Dip. Ed. talks about modern dog feeding myths. We have been raised to believe that these myths are gospel, when, in fact, they are not true and never have been.

These are the myths:

1. The digestive system of modern dog is different from that of his ancestors and therefore must be fed differently.
2. Dogs shouldn't eat bones and other raw foods.
3. All dog food should be cooked.
4. You need a university degree in dog nutrition to feed a dog.
5. The best way to feed a dog is with commercial dog food.
6. Each meal you feed a dog must be complete and balanced. [6]

Why BARF? What is BARF?

BARF is an acronym, which stands for Biologically Appropriate Raw Foods or Bones And Raw Foods. While "true" BARF feeding follows the philosophy and feeding style outlined by Dr. Billinghurst, there are several well-known people espousing feeding raw foods. Information on these different styles can be found in their books listed at the end of this article.

What are the benefits of feeding BARF?

* Healthier animals, with resulting lower veterinary costs
* Balanced energy: "hyper" animals become calmer, lethargic ones become energetic
* Naturally clean teeth
* Small, nearly odorless stools which disintegrate quickly
* Reduced chemical exposure (found in commercial foods)
* No "doggy" odor and fresh smelling breath
* Often, reversal of behavior and physical ailments
* Not yet proven, but quite likely less prone to bloat
* Less expensive
* You control what your pets eat

What are the challenges to feeding BARF?

While feeding a raw food or BARF diet to your pets is, in reality, no more complicated than feeding yourself or your family, two generations of humans have grown up listening to the commercial pet food companies' commercials. Thus we have it ingrained in our brains that feeding animals is not understandable. This indoctrination is difficult to overcome without active education about the requirements of feeding carnivores and the possible choices available. The recommendations in this article are based on Dr. Billinghurst's book(s), but, for the serious student, it is advisable to read all there is on the subject. The books at the end of this article will give a good start.

Probably the biggest challenge, after making the decision to change the way you feed your animals, is lining up your food sources. Depending on the size of your animals, a freezer may be necessary as well.

In addition, being a pioneer is never easy and there will always be well-meaning, but ill-informed family and friends and veterinarians who will try to dissuade you and will try to convince you to feed kibble again. It is often better to go ahead with your feeding changes without telling others. Once you and they see the positive changes in your animals, there will be less discussion about this.

BONES? Did you say bones and raw foods?

We've been told that bones, especially chicken bones are the very worst foods we can feed our animal companions. Where did this information come from? It came from the habit of cooking our own food and feeding the leftover bones to our animals. Cooked bones are dried out and tend to splinter, making them prime candidates for perforating digestive organs on their way through. Raw, meaty bones, however, are soft and pliable. You will be amazed at how well the carnivore jaw is adapted to eat raw bones. In fact, my Great Dane can chew up a chicken wing in 10 seconds, my Whippet can do it in 30, but it took my disposal 5 minutes to accomplish the same task! Dogs and cats are truly designed by Mother Nature to eat in this fashion.

What about salmonella & other bacteria?

Bacteria are everywhere. We all live with a tremendous amount of bacteria. Dogs and cats are especially adapted to be able to handle ingesting bacteria. Remember how these beings clean themselves!

Yes, salmonella is found on chicken, but it is also on vegetables, on your counters, your floors, in your back yard, at the park and everywhere else. What is the answer to minimizing your family's exposure to these critters? Wash your hands! Clean your counters and just be aware. Common sense and proper food handling is always advised.

Is feeding BARF safe?

Life is not "safe"; all choices carry risk. I've heard of dogs choking and dying on kibble and I've heard of dogs choking on raw meaty bones (RMBs). I have also heard of people choking on food. Feeding BARF is as safe as anything else in life and, as stated above, common sense should prevail. Supervised meals are always a good idea.

What are BARF feeders feeding?

This is an introductory article and is not meant to be comprehensive, thus the strong recommendation to read the books mentioned at the end of this article, however, I can tell you what I feed my dogs.

* Raw meaty bones (RMBs). chicken, lamb, pork, beef, fish, rabbit, venison
* Ground or chunked meats of the same animals
* Organ meats.
* Pulverized vegetables. leafy greens, squashes, broccoli, cauliflower, cabbage, carrots, beets, etc, etc. Pat McKay, in her book <u>Reigning Cats & Dogs</u> has an excellent section on the vegetables, which to feed in moderation and which are good for various conditions.
* Fruits. I feed these very rarely, mostly because I don't eat many myself. If you're eating fruit, share it with your pets. Many cats reportedly love melon!
* Seeds & nuts. almonds, pumpkin seeds, flax seeds, sunflower seeds, tahini, filberts
* Oils. primarily flaxseed oil and fish body oil. These oils help balance the fact that chicken skin is high in omega 6 fatty acids. The oils are high in omega 3's. I also feed cod liver oil in the winter since there is very little sun exposure in New England (USA) in the winter.
* Eggs with the shells.

* Concentrated whole foods (usually considered supplements) such as Super Blue Green Algae (SBGA), Aphanizomenon flos-aquae species harvested by the Cell Tech company and obtainable from independent distributors. I make a "healthy powder" consisting of SBGA, garlic, vitamin C and rotating herbs.

  Some people feed alfalfa and kelp in place of the SBGA, but I don't believe that animals with healthy thyroid glands should eat kelp everyday. In addition, the quality of both the alfalfa and the kelp is so variable that sometimes it's useless. Wherever man intervenes, you must be vigilant and know your sources

* Dairy products- these are not a part of a strict diet where the goal is to mimic the prey animal a carnivore would eat in the wild. However, they are often favorites among dogs. They provide a few probiotics (see below) and offer some variety. I feed yogurt and cottage cheese on a very occasional basis.

* Probiotics and digestive enzymes. Some people argue that these are not necessary when feeding a raw diet. Theoretically, these people are right, but reality is that most of us are buying our raw materials from grocery stores. Who knows where these foods come from and how long ago they were shipped? In this day and age, even an organic raw diet can't be depended on to provide all the nutrients. Acid rain, depleted soil, poor eating habits, stress, someone in the household smoking, etc., all contribute to less than optimum use of the foods we're feeding.

Probiotics. These are the good bacteria which populate the gut and are needed to digest some foods as well as to manufacture certain vitamins such as vitamin K (for clotting). They have a lot of other jobs as well. They are fragile and need to be replaced regularly.

Digestive Enzymes. We were taught in high school biology that our bodies make digestive enzymes—some in the mouth, some in the stomach and some in the pancreas. This is true. It is also true that those who eat a raw diet get enzymes in their food, however, when the quality of that food is compromised, we must once again draw on the body's capacity to make enzymes from the foods we eat. When the amino acids are used to make digestive enzymes, they are not then available to make other enzymes used in other functions, or to be used to run the body. Therefore, I believe that it is prudent to supplement with digestive enzymes. This is especially true for the initial transition to a raw diet, for sick or debilitated animals and for those not eating organic raw foods from known sources.

Table scraps. My dogs like to lick the plates before they go in the dishwasher and I like to let them do it. There is no harm in letting dogs have some of your food, even cooked, if you use common sense on amounts and remember that cooked bones are never included.

What about a balanced diet?

Here's what Randy Wysong, DVM has to say about a "complete and balanced diet":

"A 100% complete processed diet requires:
1.   100% complete knowledge of food.
2.   100% complete knowledge of nutrition.
3.   100% complete knowledge of #1 & #2 requires 100% complete knowledge of every science.
4.   Since #1,2 & 3 are not possible, the 100% complete processed diet is a myth." [7]

So, even if the bag says "complete and balanced", it's not likely that is what you're feeding your pet. The truth is, though, that the body knows what it needs. If you supply variety in the form of a species appropriate diet, you do not have to concern yourself about this aspect of feeding. Balance is achieved over time, not in every meal or even every day.

Dr. Ian Billinghurst does give some guidelines in his books. He suggests that 60-80% of the diet consist of RMBs. This means for every 10 meals you serve, 6-8 should be RMB meals. People achieve this in various ways and what you end up doing depends on what fits best into your lifestyle and how well your animals do on that system.

How do I know how much to feed?

I attended a Billinghurst seminar when he was lecturing in the USA in 1998. In answer to this question, he showed a slide. One side showed a drawing of a dog with her ribs sticking out. Under this drawing it said, "Feed More". The other drawing on the slide was that of an extremely obese dog and the caption said, "Feed Less." This is the simplest way to decide: let your animals tell you by how they look and feel. A healthy dog should have just the hint of visible ribs. For those who need figures, 2-3% of body weight has been suggested for adult dogs with 10% for growing puppies.

Can I feed a combination of BARF and commercial foods?

The purists would tell you that you can not, because cooked, grain-based foods are digested at a different rate from raw foods and you will create digestive upsets if you try. However, for 29 of the 31 years I have been raising dogs, I did just that. My dogs have always been fed raw foods along with kibble and they did reasonably well as far as their overall health was concerned. However, I can tell you that when I learned about BARF and completely dropped the kibble from my dogs' diets, there was a visible improvement in their coats and musculature.

Some people transition from commercial foods to BARF by alternating meals or days. There is no hard and fast rule. Do what works for you and for your animals.

What else is important when feeding my companion animals?

Finally, no discussion of diet is complete without the mention of pure water. After oxygen, water is the most important nutrient required by our bodies. Bodies are reported to be about 75% water. Therefore, it is important to provide the best quality. Quality water used to be something we could take for granted, but no more! Municipal sources are often polluted, and then sanitized by using the toxic chemical chlorine. People say to me, "but I have well water!" as though not knowing the source of our water somehow makes it better! Are you certain that underground aquifer is pristine? Are you downhill from your neighbor's septic system? The only thing better about well water is that no chlorine or fluoride has been added. Beyond that, we don't really know what's in it, and the standard water analysis which proclaims our water "safe" doesn't begin to test of the number of possible contaminants.

The only way we can be sure our water is pure is by purifying it ourselves. Water purifiers come in a variety of categories from small countertop models to whole house units. My information says that the best kind is a reverse osmosis unit. Don't be fooled into thinking that a carbon filter on the faucet is enough. Bottled water from the grocery store may be an expedient compromise in the short-term, either during the transition to a home purifier or while traveling, but this industry is little regulated and you could be drinking someone else's tap water!

Incidentally, water is also known as the universal solvent, which means that it has the ability to dissolve materials and incorporate them into itself. That plastic water dish you let water sit in all day is a toxic waste dump! Use only stainless steel or glass for your animal's food and water dishes, please!

Water quality is such a critical issue when looking at overall health, and we have been lulled for so many years into believing in the safety of our water supply, that we find it easy to just ignore this part, thinking that it doesn't pertain to us. For your own health and that of your animals, do something about your water quality today.

By combining a BARF diet with purified water and wholesome supplements, you can take steps towards ensuring that your animal companion can live a long, healthful life as nature intended.

References & Notes:

1. Give Your Dog a Bone, Ian Billinghurst, BV. Sc (Hons), B.Sc. Agr., Dip. Ed.
2. Grow Your Pups With Bones, Ian Billinghurst, BV. Sc (Hons), B.Sc. Agr., Dip. Ed.
3. Natural Nutrition: The Ultimate Diet for Dogs & Cats - Kymythy Schultze
4. Reigning Cats & Dogs - Pat McKay
5. The Complete Herbal Book for the Dog, Juliette de Bairacli Levy
6. The Holistic Guide for a Healthy Dog, Wendy Volhard & Kerry Brown, DVM
7. Natural Health for Dogs & Cats, Richard H. Pitcairn, DVM, PhD & Susan Hubble Pitcairn

* "Carbohydrates
"There is no known minimum dietary carbohydrate requirement for either the dog or the cat. Based on investigations in the dog and with other species it is likely that dogs and cats can be maintained without carbohydrates if the diet supplies enough fat or protein from which the metabolic requirement for glucose is derived."

113

-The Waltham Book of Dog & Cat Nutrition, 2nd Edition (1988)

****

"...dogs experience digestive and metabolic limitations to high grain diets, which reflect their evolution on diets relatively low in soluble carbohydrates (Clarke et al. 1990, Kronfeld 1973, Sprouse et al. 1987, White et al. 1993.)

"The nutritional strategy of carbohydrate loading risks a variety of abnormalities in dogs...An alternative strategy of fat adaptation (the combination of fat feeding and training) was found to improve aerobic performance in dogs...and to spare glycogen utilization and reduce lactate accumulation."

"More attention was given to side effects in dogs and horses, species that did not evolve on high grain diets. Attempts at carbohydrate loading led to tying up, a mild form of exertional rhabdomyolysis in racing sled dogs (Kronfeld 1973)."

-Kronfeld et al. 1994. Optimal Nutrition for Athletic Performance, with Emphasis on Fat Adaptation in Dogs and Horses. The Journal of Nutrition 124:2745s-2753s.

****

"Provided the diet contains sufficient glucose precursors (amino acids and glycerol), the glucogenic capacity of the liver and kidneys is usually sufficient to meet the metabolic need of growing animals for glucose without the inclusion of carbohydrate in the diet (Brambia and Hill, 1966; Chen et al., 1980)."

-Nutrient Requirements of Dogs, Rev. 1985. National Academy of Sciences

****

1   Mammal Species of the World: A Taxonomic and Geographic Reference, edited by D.E. Wilson and D.A.M. Reeder
2   BARF email list at egroups.com
3   Canine Health Naturally Newsletter, Sandra Brigola
4   Natural Rearing Newsletter, Marina Zacharias
5   Food Pets Die For, Ann Martin
6   Give Your Dog A Bone,
7   Fresh & Whole:Getting Involved In Your Pet's Diet,Randy Wysong, DVM

Betty Lewis, RVT, Dr. A.N.

.

Nutrition (again)

If you were told that after weaning, you should feed your child nothing but Total Cereal for the rest of its life (100% complete nutrition, right?), what would you think? Could you imagine a life without fresh foods? Could you imagine eating the same thing meal after meal, day after day, forever?

What if your child were designed to eat raw meat and all you ever gave it was cooked cereal? How long is it likely to assume that it would remain healthy in body, mind, and spirit?

Pet food companies would like us to believe that we should feed our pets the same devitalized, cooked concoctions day in and day out. However, common sense, at the very least, should make us take another look.

"But dogs and cats are *domesticated* animals," you say. They've *evolved* to eat processed foods. This is a myth and patently untrue. They have been "domesticated" for at least the past 5,000 years, but processed pet foods have only existed for the past 60 or so years. In sixty years, our carnivorous pets did not evolve to live on artificial food. They still share the digestive system with wild carnivores, and it is to *them* that we should look for guidance.

The first deficiency of a totally processed diet is that it is cooked. Have you ever seen any of the animals depicted on the nature TV shows cooking their meals? Barring forest fires, wild carnivores do not eat cooked foods. Their digestive systems are designed to eat primarily meat, and to eat it raw. In consuming whole animals, these wild animals get all the nutrients necessary to build their own systems. They get meat, bone, roughage and the vegetable contents of the prey's stomach. Except for the vegetable content which is "minimally processed" inside of the prey, all of the food is uncooked.

The next problem with depending on commercial products is that the quality of the ingredients is not what the TV commercials would lead you to believe. In addition to the 4-D

117

meats (dead, diseased, dying & disabled), there are a host of other inedibles all cooked to render them sterile and then packed with chemical preservatives.

This isn't about what *not* to do, so I will refer now to several wonderful books which can take this subject much farther and give you guidance in how to proceed appropriately.

1. *Give Your Dog a Bone*, Ian Billinghurst, DVM
2. *Reigning Cats & Dogs*, Pat McKay
3. *The Ultimate Diet*, Kymythy Schultze

The *best* way to feed both dogs and cats is 100% home-prepared food. It is not necessary to feed every meal "complete and balanced". The very thought that this is an achievable goal is unrealistic, anyway. It would only be possible to create something 100% complete if we *knew* 100% about the subject. Since no one knows 100% about chemistry or nature, we shouldn't be taken in by the myth that this is possible.

It's not the way we feed ourselves, either. As we do for ourselves, we should be providing a variety of raw foods and allow our pet's body, in its innate wisdom, to choose the nutrients it needs. We only need to remember that while humans require the balance to be tipped in favor of plant matter, carnivores require more animal matter. Both of us need both varieties though.

Further, it has never been proven that carnivorous pets require grains (carbohydrates) at all! The reason there is so much corn, wheat, rice, and other grains in pet foods is purely economic! It's cheaper to feed grains than meat and vegetables, but it isn't *better*! It's also true that pet food companies began as outlets for the waste products of the baking industry and the thinking has never changed.

The books listed above can help you to feed your new puppy or kitten from the beginning, supplying healthy raw ingredients.

For those who find this too radical a change all at once, it is possible to use a high quality, all natural pet food as *long as you supplement with raw foods in addition.* After a home prepared BARF diet, a commercial raw diet, either fermented or frozen is the best choice.

If you must use a commercial product that has been cooked, be aware that this is a significant compromise to your animals' health. However, here are some guidelines to consider when selecting a cooked commercial food:

1. The first ingredient should be from an animal source. This can be misleading, however. If there are three or four grain sources in the next few ingredients, the food is obviously a grain-based food once you add these together, not an animal-based one. Further, pet food labels list the ingredients by weight. "Chicken" for example, is weighed with all the water in it. After removing the water, there might not be much chicken actually in the food. "Chicken meal" would be a more desirable ingredient to have listed first.

2. If any one or more of these ingredients are present, it is reason to reject the entire food: BHA, BHT, ethoxyquin, beet pulp or propylene glycol.

3. The bag should be dated. Only buy freshly manufactured foods.

Remember that the cliche "you are what you eat" has its basis in fact. If you feed your animals dead, diseased, and devitalized foods, you cannot support life, health, and vitality.

Betty Lewis, RVT, Dr. A.N.

Appendix III

The Predator/Prey Relationship

I have been asked, "From the point of view of the animals, is it wrong for humans to eat other species?"

Over the years, I have gone to the source and put this question to numerous animals, both wild and domestic. Each time, I receive the same basic answer. First, there is total astonishment that I should be asking such a question. Then these statements have come to me from different sources: "That's the way it is in all of nature," they said. "Some eat plants, others eat the plant eaters. That's recycling at its most efficient! Why do you think we come to serve you in this form? Why would we come in this form if we were no use to you?"

Whether I queried chickens, sheep, lobsters or cats, hawks or insect-eating birds, the answer was the same. Part of the law of nature revolves around the predator/prey relationship. All take part.

The critical part of this relationship, which some humans have forgotten, is that this is an agreement between predator and prey and because of this it is necessary for the predator to respect the prey. Sometimes it seems that the predator even reveres the prey. Sometimes the act appears to be a ritual with consent on both sides. I asked a mouse who was being played with by a cat why he didn't run when he had the chance? He said that he had agreed to be dinner and it was okay. It has always been the custom of Native Americans to thank the spirit of the animal being hunted for the gift of its body. This is a custom we could well adopt prior to a meat meal.

Animals gladly give up their bodies to serve our species, but in return they request a good life. I have a neighbor who annually raises a steer for slaughter. His life is short, but it is such a pleasant one that the person would be astounded to know he raises the same animal year after year! Animals who are

121

raised for slaughter have agreed to provide themselves for our food. They do not, however, deserve pain and fear as they die. It is up to us as their guardians to allow them dignity in death and to appreciate with our thanks the nourishment they freely give us.

Appendix IV

Cleaning Up Your Act

Often things are not as they seem. I have learned never to presume that I know what is causing a problem until I speak to the animals. No matter how obvious the answer may seem, it's just a guess until you ask the source.

Janice called me saying her cat had "allergies." Ripley was pulling out her hair and Janice wanted to know how she could treat her to stop this behavior. I asked Ripley how she was feeling, expecting to get answers revolving around itching or something physical or emotional. What I learned was that Ripley had come to this person to protect her from a toxic environment. Her intention was literally to absorb the toxins herself so that her person would be spared. This was a very nice gesture, but since both were living in the environment, both were absorbing the same toxins. It just showed up sooner in the cat. Another approach was needed. Our attention then turned to various ways to lessen toxic exposure in the home.

We discussed cat nutrition first as a way to start Ripley on the road back to health. The importance of raw, animal-based food was discussed. Pure water also took time in our attention. I recommend a reverse osmosis purifier and that only pure water be used for cooking and drinking.

Parasiticides are a big factor in cleaning up an environment where animals reside. This was not a factor in her case, but a topic that must be included for many households.

A critical area that is regularly misunderstood is the use of cleaning and disinfectant products. We are so bombarded with commercials about cleaning products that we start to take them for granted. Some of the most common ones are the most toxic. Products ending in "-sol" are some of the prime offenders and are particularly harmful to cats.

Baking soda is an effective replacement for many powdered cleansers and I find it takes stains out of kitchen counters better than the poisonous commercial products.

There are some commercial lines out there with safe products, too. Explore these by calling the companies and asking them what sets their products apart and why you should use them. Talk to people in the health food stores also, as they sell non-toxic cleaning products and often use them personally.

By providing a safer environment, you eliminate problems for your animals, the earth, and yourself. Ripley wasn't able to take on all the toxins into herself, but her timely call for help has set the whole family on the road to greater health.

Appendix V

Resources

Newsletters/Periodicals

American Veterinary Chiropractic
Association Newsletter
623 Main St
Hillsdale, IL 61257
309-658-2920
Sharon Willoughby, DVM,DC
$35/yr

Best Friends Magazine
Best Friends Animal Sanctuary
Kanab, UT 84741-5001
801-644-2001
bestfriends@msn.com
Editor: Michael Mountain
$25/yr/ 10 issues

Canine Health Naturally
POB 69
Lions Bay, BC Canada VON2EO
sandra@anionet.com
Editor: Sandra Brigola
$20/yr/6 issues

Canine Health Concern
POB 1
Lognor, Derbyshire, England SK170JD
$25/year

Betty Lewis, RVT, Dr. A.N.

Convergence
One Sanborn Rd
Concord, NH 03301

Healthy Pets Naturally
1895 New Franklin Church Rd
Canon, GA 30520
706-356-7031

Holistic Animal Care Newsletter
on line at deerhounds@aol.com

Holistic Horse
115 15th St
Surf City, NJ 08008
609-494-4215
$12/yr/4 issues

Homeopathy Today
National Center for Homeopathy
801 N. Fairfax St, Suite 306
Alexandria, VA 22314
703-548-7790
nchinfo@icg.apc.org
http://www.healthy.net/nch
$40/yr/11 issues
$6 practioner directory

Iternational Veterinary Accupuncture
Society (IVAS)
POB 2074
Nederland, CO 80466
303-258-3767
$40/yr/2 issues each of Veterinary Accupuncture Journal &
IVAS Newsletter

Journal of the American Holistic Veterinary
Medical Association
2214 Old Emmorton Rd.
BelAir, MD 21014
410-569-0795
http://www.altvetmed.com
$65/yr/4 issues

Love of Animals
7811 Montrose Rd
Potomac, MD 20854
301-424-3700

Natural Reared Animal Directory
245 Lakeview Lane
Murphy, NC 28906
704-837-8019
umerski@dnet.net
free listing
directory $11.90

Natural Rearing Newsletter
POB 1436
Jacksonville, OR 97530
ambrican@cdsnet.net
Editor: Marina Zacharias
$19/yr/6 issues

Price-Pottenger Health Journal
2667 Camino del Rio So. Suite 109
San Diego, CA 92108-3767
800-FOODS-4-U
info@price-pottenger.org
http://www.price-pottenger.org
$35donation/yr/4 issues

Species Link; Journal of Interspecies
Telepathic Communication
POB 1060
Point Reyes, CA94956
800-242-0036
Editor: Penelope Smith
$25/yr/4 issues

TTEAM Connections
5435 Rochdell Rd
Vernon, BC VIBE8CN
TTEAM office 800-854-TEAM
$24/yr /6 issues

Whole Dog Journal
POB 420032
Palm Coast, FL 32142-0032
$20/yr/12 issues

Wysong Companion Animal Health Letter
1880 North Eastman
Midland, MI 48640-8896
517-631-0009

Holistic Organizations

Academy of Veterinary Homeopathy
1283 Lincoln St
Eugene, OR 97401
541-342-7665
Send $2 & SASE for listing of AVH certified veterinarians

American Holistic Veterinary
Medical Association
2214 Old Emmorton Rd.
BelAir, MD 21015
410-569-0795
http://www.altvetmed.com
AHVMA@compuserve.com

American Veterinary Chiropractic Association
Sharon Willoughby, DVM,DC
623 Main St.
Hillsdale, IL 61257
309-658-2920
$35 for Friends of the AVCA membership
Send SASE for list of graduates

Center for Veterinary Acupuncture
Maria Glinski, DVM
1405 West Silver Spring Dr.
Glendale, WI 53209
800-680-2282
SASE for graduate list

Flower Essence Society
POB 459
Nevada City, CA 95959
916-265-9163
$20/yr

International Association for Veterinary Homeopathy
Susan Wynn, DVM
334 Knollwood Lane
Woodstock, GA 30188
770-516-7622
swynn@emory.edu
SASE for list of courses & members

International Veterinary Acupuncture Society (IVAS)
POB 2074
Nederland, CO 80466
303-258-3767
SASE for directory

National Center for Homeopathy
901 N. Fairfax St, Suite 306
Alexandria, VA 22314
703-548-7790
nchinfo@icg.apc.org
http://www.healthy.net/nch
$6 for info including directory

Natural Pet Products Association
POB 355
Conner, MT 59827
406-821-1939

Veterinary Institute for Therapeutic Alternatives
Allen Schoen, DVM
15 Sunset Terrace
Sherman, CT 06784
860-354-2287
SASE for graduate list

Books-Telepathic Communication

Animal Talk - Penelope Smith
Animals...Our Return to Wholeness- Penelope Smith
Animal Wisdom, Communication with Animals- Anita Curtis
Kinship With All Life- J. Allen Boone
Communication With Animals: The Spiritual Connection
Between People and Animals-Arthur Myers
Talking With Nature- Michael Roads
What the Animals Tell Me- Beatrice Lydecker

Stories Animals Tell Me- Beatrice Lydecker
Animals As Teachers and Healers- Susan Chermack McElroy

Books- Holistic Health

Are You Poisoning Your Pets? - Nina Anderson & Howard Peiper
Complimentary & Alternative Veterinary Medicine- Allen Schoen, DVM &n Susan Wynn, DVM
Cat Care, Naturally- Celeste Yarnall, PhD
Cats Naturally: Natural Rearing for Healthier Cats- Juliette de Bairacli Levy
Dr. Pitcairn's Complete Guide to Natural Health for Dogs & Cats- Richard Pitcairn, DVM, PhD and Susan Hubble Pitcairn
Four Paws, Five Directions- Cheryl Schwartz, DVM
Herbal Remedies for Dogs & Cats: A Pocket Guide- Mary Wulff-Tilford & Gregory Tilford
How to Have a Healthier Dog- Wendell O. Bellfield, DVM & Martin Zucker
Keep Your Pet Healthy the Natural Way- Pat Lazarus
Love, Miracles & Animal Healing- Allen Schoen, DVM
Natural Healing for Dogs & Cats- Diane Stein
The Natural Remedy Book for Dogs & Cats- Diane Stein
Natural Immunity- Pat McKay
Natural Insect Repellants- Janette Grainger & Connie Moore
The Complete Herbal Book for the Dog & Cat- Juliette de Bairacli Levy
The Holistic Guide for a Healthy Dog- Wendy Volhard & Kerry Brown,DVM
The Holistic Veterinary Handbook, Will Winter, DVM
The New Natural Cat- Anitra Frazier
The Tellington Touch- Linda Tellington-Jones
The Well Adjusted Dog & The Well Adjusted Cat- Daniel Kamen, DC
The New Holistic Herbal- David hoffman

131

Books- Homeopathy & Flower Essences

A Veterinary Materia Medica & Clinical Repertory- George Macleod, MRCVS, DVSM
Cats: Homeopathic Remedies- George Macleod, MRCVS, DVSM
Dogs: Homeopathic Remedies- George Macleod, MRCVS, DVSM
The Homeopathic Treatment of Small Animals: Principles & Practice- Christopher Day, MRCVS, MA Vet MB,
Vet MF Hom
The Treatment of Cats by Homeopathy- K. Sheppard
Flower Essence Repertory- Patricia Kaminski & Richard Katz
Flower Remedies Handbook-Donna Cunningham
Flower Essences- Machaelle Small Wright
Handbook of the Bach Flower Remedies- Philip M. Chancellor
Bach Flower Therapy- Mechthild Scheffer
Flowers to the Rescue- Gregory Vlamis
The Bach Flower Remedies-Edward Bach, MD

Books- Nutrition

AAFCO Publication
Georgia Dept of Agriculture
Room 604, Capitol Square
Atlanta, GA 30334
404-656-3637

Aqua Vitae: Catalyst Altered Water- Roy Jacobsen
Food Pets Die For- Ann Martin
Give Your Dog a Bone- Ian Billinghurst, B V.Sc
It's For the Animals! Cookbook- Helen L. McKinnon
Natural Nutrition: The Ultimate Diet for Dogs & Cats- Kymythy Schultze
Reigning Cats & Dogs- Pat McKay
Super Nutrition for Animals- Nina Anderson & Howard Peiper

Suppliers

A Drop in the Bucket- Herbs
586 Round Hill Rd
Greenwich, CT 06831
888-783-0313

Marina Zacharias-variety
POB 1436 Jacksonville, OR 97530
541-899-2080
ambrican@cdsnet.net

Animals Apawthecary- Herbs
POB 212
Conner, MT 59827
406-821-4090

Dogwise
POB 2778
701B Poplar
Wenatchee, WA 98807-2778
800-776-2665
http://www.dogwise.com

Dolisos-Homeopathics
3014 Rigel Ave
Las Vegas, NV 89102
800-DOLISOS

Ellon Bach, USA- Bach Flower Remedies
644 Merrick Rd.
Lynbrook, NY 11563
800-433-7523

Fleabusters Rx for Fleas-flea removal
10801 National Boulevard
Los Angeles, Ca 90064
800-846-3532

Flower Essence Services- non Bach flower essences
POB 1769
Nevada City, CA 95959
800-548-0075

Frontier Cooperative Herbs
POB 299
Norway, IA 52318
800-786-1388

Halo-variety
3438 East Lake Rd. #14
Palm Harbor, FL 34685
800-426-4256

HoBoN- Homeovetics
POB 8243
Naples, FL 33941
800-521-7722

Homeopathic Educational Services
2124 Kittredge St.
Berkeley, CA 94704
800-359-9051

Morrill's New Directions-variety
POB 30
Orient, ME 04471
800-368-5057

Norfields Magnetics
632 3/4 No. Doheny Dr.
Los Angeles, CA 90069
800-344-8400

Pat McKay, Inc.-variety
396 W. Washington Blvd
Pasadena, CA 91103
800-975-7555

Pet's Friend, Inc.-variety
7154 No. Univeersity Dr., Suite 720
Tamarac, FL 33221
800-868-1009

Petsage-herbs
4313 Wheeler Ave
Alexandria, VA 22304
800- PET-HEALTH

Standard Homeopathics
POB 61067
Los Angeles, CA 90061
800
624-9659

The Minimum Price- homeopathic books
POB 2187
Blaine, WA 98231
800-663-8272

Resources on-Line
Animal Communication

Animal Connection
http://www.CyberArk.com/animal/animalcn.htm

Health & Medical Information

Red Branch Irish Wolfhounds
http://home.fianet/~marshaw/health.htm
AHVMA http://www.altvetmed.com
Shirley's Wellness Cafe
http://www.geocities.com/HotSprings/1158/animals.htm
Jean Dodds' articles-
http://av.yahoo.com/bin/query?p=Dodds%2C+jean&hc=0&hs=0
Vaccination in animals
http://www.healthy.net/library/articles/ivn/animals.h=tm
Abbey wood publishing
http://members.aol.com/abywood/www/art_toc.htm
Cyberpet
http://cyberpet.com/cyberdog/articles/health/vaccin.htm
They Shoot Horses but Vaccinate dogs (and children)
http://www.positivehealth.com/Bakissue/horses.htm

Vaccines and Sarcomas:
http://www.avma.org/vafstf/ownbroch.html
The Dangers of Vaccinations, and the Advantages of Nosodes
for Disease
Prevention http://www.abap.org/nosodes.htm
Homeopath doctor
http://www.naturalholistic.com/handouts/hpmaster.htm
Loops D.V.M.- nosodes-
http://www.gld.com/~shrado/loops.htm
Mehan DVM http://www.abap.org/nosodes.htm
Grapefruit Seed Extract-
http://www.sover.net/%7Esamallen/more.htm#GSE

Nutrition Information

Ann Martin's article
http://www.peg.apc.org/~nexus/Petfood.html
Kathy Partridge's article

http://www.dreamscape.com/grccny/food_html.html
Andrea Madeley's article
http://www.albany.net/~sterling/bones.htm
Tom Lonsdale, DVM http://www.zeta.org.au/~lonsdale/
API Pet Food Report
http://209.1.224.11/HotSprings/1158/PETFOOD.HTM
Linda Arndt's articles
http://www.DogLogic.com/arndtindex.htm

Homeopathy/Flower Essences

http://home.earthlink.net/~fourwinds/homeopathy.html
http://www.homevet.com/
http://www.lyghtforce.com/HomeopathyOnline/
http://www.ihr.com/homeopat/index.html
http://www.homeopathy.com/
http://www.indiaspace.com/homoeopathy/
http://www.Medicinegarden.com/
http://www.bachcentre.com/index.html
http://www2.bitstream.net/~bunlion/bpi/FeArt.html
http://www.flowersociety.org/
http://www.gld.com/~shrado/homeopat.htm?
Repertory-http://www.islandnet.com/~wildlife/reper.html#39

Homeopathic Pharmacies

Dolisos 800-DOLISOS
Washington Homeopathic 800-336-1695
Homeopathy Overnight 800-ARNICA 30
Mid America Homeopathic Medicine Shop 800-552-4956
Standard Homeopathic 800-624-9659
Boiron/Borneman 800-BLU TUBE

Holistic Practitioners

http://www.altvetmed.com/ahvmadir.html
http://home.earthlink.net/~fourwinds/index.html
http://www.naturalholistic.com/
http://www.healthmall.com/

Holistic Mail Lists

Athena: Athena-request@MedicineGarden.com
Wellpet: Majordomo@ListService.net
Go to www.eGroups.com and www.smartGroups.com for more mailing lists than you could eve wish for.

Supplies

Morrill's New Directions- http://www.morrills.com
Pat McKay- http://home1.gte.net/patmckay/index.html
Dogwise-http://www.dogwise.com
TTEAM/Tellington Touch- http://lindatellingtonjones.com/

Betty Lewis, RVT, Dr. A. N.
17 Danbury Circle
Amherst, NH 03031
603-673-3263

Betty Lewis, RVT, Dr. A.N. is a graduate of the College of Wooster (Russian, Spanish & Secondary Education), Maple Woods Community College (Veterinary Technology) and Trinity School of Natural Health (Naturopathy). She worked in veterinary hospitals for 14 years before opening her consulting practice, Paws and Reflect, in 1987.

Betty lives in Amherst, NH with her husband, of 34 years, Bill, two Great Danes, Druid and Raisin and Whippets, Halo and Shimmer. She has been a Great Dane breeder/exhibitor since 1969, involved in conformation & obedience dog showing, tracking and freestyle. Lure coursing and Whippet racing are new adventures since Halo joined the family. Betty is an American Kennel Club approved judge in Great Danes and Junior Showmanship and provisional in Doberman Pinschers.

She is a member of The Great Dane Club of New England, The Great Dane Club of America, American Dog Show Judges, Senior Conformation Judges Association, The Tracking Club of Massachusetts, Ladies' Dog Club, North American Veterinary Technician's Association, Hill Country Lure Coursers and the Whippet Racing Association.

Betty has been talking with animals since 1977. Her clinical and private experience has shown her that taking the time to mentally communicate with animals enriches our association with all life.

Animals Speak! is a compilation of stories right out of Betty's case files as well as a private class in Talking With Animals, Betty's workshop program. In addition there is information to help the reader provide a healthy lifestyle for his/her companion animals.

Printed in the United States
5244

9 780759 621725